Crime Writers

Reflections on crime fiction by

Reginald Hill

P.D.James

H.R.F.Keating

Troy Kennedy Martin

Maurice Richardson

Julian Symons

Colin Watson

Edited by

H.R.F.Keating

Additional material by

Mike Pavett

British Broadcasting Corporation

This book is published in conjunction
with a series of six BBC Further Education
Television programmes *Crime Writers,*
first transmitted on BBC-1 from Sunday
5 November 1978

The series produced by Bernard Adams

Illustrations by Eric Critchley

Published to accompany a series of programmes prepared in
consultation with the BBC Further Education Advisory Council

©The Contributors 1978
First published 1978

Published by the British Broadcasting Corporation
35 Marylebone High Street, London W1M 4AA

Printed in England by Tonbridge Printers Ltd, Tonbridge, Kent
Set in 10/12pt Century Schoolbook VIP
ISBN 0 563 16263 5 (paperback)
ISBN 0 563 16287 2 (hardback)

Contents

Editor's Foreword
by H.R.F.Keating   6

Introduction: Before the fiction
by Mike Pavett   8

1 Holmes: The Hamlet of crime fiction
by Reginald Hill   20

  After Holmes†   42

2 Mayhem Parva and Wicked Belgravia
by Colin Watson   48

3 Dorothy L. Sayers: From puzzle to novel
by P.D.James   64

  From the Golden Age to Mean Streets†   76

4 Dashiell Hammett: The Onlie Begetter
by Julian Symons   80

  Other hardboiled heroes†   94

5 Simenon and Highsmith: Into the criminal's head
by Maurice Richardson   100

  Crooks and Cops†   118

6 Four of a kind?
by Troy Kennedy Martin   122

  Police stories and after†   134

7 New patents pending
by H.R.F.Keating   138

The Authors   156

Index   157

†The linking material between chapters is by Mike Pavett

Editor's Foreword

by H.R.F.Keating

Crime, the breaking of the laws, has always exercised a fascination over the human mind. In order to live together in societies, one of the marks of humankind, it is necessary to have laws, but inevitably such laws restrict. They prevent us doing all that it is in our nature to do. So, though we recognise and even applaud them, we also hate them, a little or very much. Writers, storytellers, through the ages have been able to give expression to this hate, though it is only in comparatively recent times, thanks to mechanical advances like the invention of cheap printing, that what could be called a literature of crime has come to be.

But, once begun, that literature for, I think, the reasons I have indicated flourished exceedingly. It is now the subject, very properly, of a BBC Television Further Education series.

Here in the form of words on the page and still pictures is another study of the theme of that series. It has the same title. It has a high proportion of the same contributors. It even uses some of the same interview material. Its aim is broadly the same. But it is not those programmes put into a more easily consulted form. It is something different.

Television has its own way of conveying information: books, even illustrated ones, go about conveying it in another manner. So, although in editing this volume I have kept loosely to the format which Bernard Adams, the producer of the television series, devised together with Mike Pavett, the writer for the programmes, I have expected the authors whom I asked to contribute the essays to approach their various subjects in at the least a slightly different way. Not only have they been in a position to lay down more facts than the television programmes could in their necessarily short length, but they have too, almost inevitably, taken somewhat different views of their subjects, if only because they could treat them in a wider and more subtle manner.

Yet the general aim has been the same. We have not set out to produce primarily a history of crime writing, chronicling how one writer influenced another, how some rebelled against the dictates of their predecessors. That has been done already and admirably, first a good many years ago in America by Howard Haycraft in his *Murder for Pleasure,* more recently in Britain by Julian Symons in *Bloody Murder: from the detective story to the crime novel: a history.*

Instead, we have tried to look at crime and the writer. We have asked ourselves how at various periods the writers of the day tackled their subject. We have asked what readers, and later viewers, wanted from them. Our approach has tended to be more social commentary than literary history.

So we have perhaps put less emphasis on the work of some authors than of others. There may be names (your very own favourite) completely omitted who in another context would be major figures. And indeed, even with the advantage of the space we have, there have certainly been writers we have had to omit or barely refer to who might have been thought to have earned prescriptive mention even under our particular terms of reference. But to have produced a work that was no more than lists of authors, however worthy, would have been self-defeating. We would not have been able to say much about crime writing and crime writers, and crime readers. And I hope we have done that.

The editor of a book such as this is like a spider. He sits there in the early stages spinning an aerial web of suggestions, promises, even sticky flatteries, and he hopes eventually to catch a full haul of meaty flies, perhaps a succulent bumblebee or a dragonfly for his deep-freeze. I think I have been enormously lucky in the haul I caught, and I am very grateful to my fellow contributors for allowing themselves to be enmeshed in my silvery filaments. And I am yet more grateful to Bernard Adams, whose original conception both television series and book were. He, together with Mike Pavett who has also contributed substantially to the pages that follow as well as finding many if not all the illustrations, built the substantial walls from which I later swung my threads and made my web. I trust the result will be both stimulating and informative for all who come to look at it.

Introduction: Before the Fiction

by Mike Pavett

Crime fascinates us. It has been estimated that about a quarter of all fiction sold in England and America is crime fiction. But in spite of its large and devoted following crime is a comparative newcomer to the world of fiction, an upstart of dubious parentage.

Before crime fiction existed as such there had been a steadily increasing demand, especially from the literate sections of the working class, for cheaply produced topical and sensational material. Broad sheets and ballads giving highly coloured accounts of crimes and executions made up a large proportion of the printers' output.

The eighteenth century was a time of great social changes in Britain; among them were the spread of literacy and the availability of cheap printed material of all kinds, together with the first attempts at forming an organised police force. The London of that time was reputed to have been one of the most violent and lawless cities in Europe. The concentration of wealth in 'the City' was surrounded by the tottering labyrinths of squalid and insanitary housing where the poorest of London's inhabitants lived. For many of them crime became a means of survival, an alternative to real poverty and hunger. In this environment crime grew unchecked, for there was virtually no official police force. Parts of London were patrolled by private watch services, others by elderly night watchmen and an assortment of street-keepers, marshalmen, beadles and other generally untrained and ineffective keepers of the peace.

The first attempt at any organised policing was made by Jonathan Wild. When he proclaimed himself 'Thief Taker General of Britain and Ireland' there were many who were only too pleased that someone should undertake such a seemingly impossible task and were willing to let him go about his business as he saw fit. In spite of his grandiose title Wild effectively controlled only London, but his influence was profound. He set about the business of detecting criminals and recovering stolen goods by building up a network of informers. As he was self-appointed he received no salary but depended on the rewards that he received. This led to accusations that he bought stolen goods in

· JONATHAN WILD THIEF-TAKER GENERAL OF GREAT BRITTAIN & IRELAND ·

order to claim the reward for their return, and also that he even arranged the theft. He certainly traded with and encouraged those criminals who co-operated with him, though he was not averse to arresting and giving evidence against them once they had achieved sufficient notoriety for the reward to be worthwhile. These practices earned him the popular nickname of 'Thief Maker'.

Wild's dual role eventually came to light, and he was hanged in 1725, but by that time he had brought a degree of order, if not of law, to London. Gang violence had almost disappeared from the city, and highwaymen had ceased to operate in the London area. In spite of these achievements his end was welcomed by many. A ballad published on the day of his execution contained the couplet:

Now Devil take thy Darling Wild
He's been thy servant since a Child.

To all the Thieves, Whores, Pick-pockets, Family Fellons &c. in Great Brittain & Ireland. Gentlemen & Ladies, You are hereby desir'd to accompany y.ᵉ worthy friend y.ᵉ Pious M.ʳ I— W—d from his Seat at Whittingtons Colledge to y.ᵉ Tripple Tree, where he's to make his last Exit on   , and his Corps to be Carry'd from thence to be decently Interr'd a=mongst his Ancestors.

Pray bring this Ticket with you.

'An Invitation' to Wild's execution

While the public rejected Wild they took Jack Sheppard to their hearts. Sheppard was a professional criminal who by his daring exploits had captured the imagination of the people. Sheppard was the honest thief, while Wild was the hypocritical arm of the law. Broad sheets and ballads of the time give a good indication of the public feeling, celebrating both Sheppard's escape and Wild's execution. Printers and publishers of the time were quick to respond to the mood. James Applebee published *A True and Genuine Account of . . . Jonathan Wild* shortly

after his execution, as he had previously done with *The History and Remarkable Life of Jack Sheppard*. The authorship of both these works has been attributed to Daniel Defoe. He certainly had a good knowledge of Wild and his circle, and made use of it in his books, particularly *Moll Flanders*.

John Gay had certainly met Wild, and based the corrupt and grasping Peachum in *The Beggar's Opera* on him. Various melodramas were based on Wild and Sheppard and, together with *The Beggar's Opera* they continued to be per-

Jack Sheppard

John Gay

formed long after the real characters had been forgotten.

After Wild's execution London was again without any organized form of police force, and corrupt magistrates like Sir Thomas de Veil made fortunes out of bribery. De Veil was succeeded by Henry Fielding, who in his satirical novel *The History of the Life of the Late Mr. Jonathan Wild the Great* had used Wild, as Swift had before him, to exemplify dishonesty and corruption. Fielding was determined to do something about the lawlessness of London, and in

1753 he founded the Bow Street Runners. With a staff of only seven men – his assistant and six constables – he laid the foundation for the modern police force. Fielding died a year later, but was succeeded by his half brother John Fielding, the 'Blind Magistrate', who carried on and greatly enlarged the scope of his work. He established police records, the exchange of information between magistrates in different areas, and recruited innkeepers, turnpikes and pawnbrokers as informants. The authority and prestige of the Bow Street Runners increased,

Bow Street Runner

(*Above*) Henry Fielding
(*below*) his half-brother John,
the blind magistrate

Part of the Catnach broadsheet describing the murder of Maria Marten

and they continued until ten years after Robert Peel established in 1829 the body from which present-day police forces are directly descended.

Although not above suspicion the Runners were the first law officers that the public regarded as heroes. In 1827 *Scenes in the Life of a Bow Street Runner, Drawn up from His Private Memoranda* was published under the name of 'Richmond'. It represents a significant shift in public sympathy. The hero is an upholder of the law and society, not a rebel. Although many subsequent writers, including Dickens, criticized and ridiculed the Runners they had been in existence for almost a hundred years and had prepared the way for the creation of a proper police force.

For much of the nineteenth century popular reading material about crime remained unchanged. The broad sheets and ballads grew in popularity. They were usually illustrated accounts of the crime, accompanied by what purported to be a true confession from the condemned cell, often written in verse. James Catnach was one of the most successful publishers, and his account of *The Murder of Maria Marten* sold over one and a half million copies. The sympathies expressed in the broad sheets had changed from those of the previous century. Although the crimes are sometimes sympathetically reported, the criminals are no longer presented as heroes.

The first policeman to become a well-known public figure was the Frenchman, Eugène François Vidocq. He was originally a criminal, and while in prison he became a police informer. He was so successful that in 1811 he was given his freedom and appointed the first Chef de la Sûreté. While not as corrupt a figure as

Eugène François Vidocq

Edgar Allan Poe

Jonathan Wild had been there are nevertheless similarities between the careers of the two men. Like Wild he received no salary, but was paid on results. This, together with the fact that most of his agents were also ex-criminals, led to him being suspected of arranging some of the crimes he solved, or at least acting as an *agent provocateur*. He was forced to resign in 1827, but was reappointed five years later. He was again forced to resign after less than a year in office. After this he worked as a private detective and occasional police informer, but, more importantly, he turned to writing.

Vidocq's memoirs are ghost-written and highly coloured, but they are firmly based on his life and experiences. A criminal turned policeman, a possibly corrupt policeman, a master of disguise mixing unrecognised with the very criminals he is hunting, Vidocq is always on the borderline between hero and villain. It was this ambiguity that gave him the power to capture the public imagination. The memoirs had a great effect on the writers of crime fiction in his own time and after.

Balzac knew Vidocq well, and used him as the basis for the policeman Vautrin in *La Comédie Humaine*.

Crime fiction as we know it appears for the first time in the works of Edgar Allan Poe. In three of his stories, 'The Murders in the Rue Morgue', 'The Mystery of Marie Roget' and 'The Purloined Letter' he created the first great detective in fiction, Chevalier C. Auguste Dupin, a man of great intelligence who solves crimes by observation and reason. These three stories are also the first examples of a locked room mystery, an armchair detective story and of the obvious solution being the best concealment. 'The Gold Bug' is a puzzle story with a cryptogram at its heart, and 'Thou Art The Man' is the first unlikeliest solution story with its deliberately misleading clues and elementary ballistics. In 'The Tell-tale Heart' and 'The Cask of Amontillado' Poe is concerned with the workings of the mind of a murderer, in one story destroyed by guilt and in the other without even the slightest feeling of remorse. These seven stories are a small part of Poe's output, but they are the

Wilkie Collins

A London policeman of the eighteen sixties

prototypes for most of the crime fiction that was to follow.

It was not until 1842, with the formation of the Detective Department of the Metropolitan Police that crime writing became an identifiable trend. This new organisation was part of the full time professional force set up by Robert Peel, not an irregular group working for reward and profit. They were less susceptible to bribery and corruption than their predecessors, and their creation was welcomed, particularly by the middle class. The working class had been traditionally hostile to the police, but this was changing as their role of keepers of the peace and not oppressors became accepted.

In popular literature the romantic image of the criminal as a hero at odds with a repressive and unjust society was gradually replaced by the new hero, the detective as the protector of society. When Charles Dickens wrote articles in *Household Words* in 1850 about the new police the public were ready to share his basic admiration for their work. Dickens was fascinated by the police, and spent time with officers as they

went about their work. He later created the first English fictional detective, Inspector Bucket in *Bleak House*, but, like Balzac he was not concerned primarily with crime but with a whole range of human types and emotions. If *The Mystery of Edwin Drood* had been finished it might perhaps have been a crime novel, but it was Dickens' friend Wilkie Collins who wrote the first successful English crime novel. Some of his early books and short stories had crime and detection as themes, but it was in *The Woman in White* and *The Moonstone* that crime became the central point of the story. Both books have intricate and ingenious plots, and Count Fosco in *The Woman in White* is one of the great villains of crime fiction, while the appearance, mannerisms and investigative methods of Sergeant Cuff in *The Moonstone* make him a memorable police detective.

The other great fictional detective is Emile Gaboriau's French policeman Lecoq. The dislike of the police was stronger in France, but, as in England this was changing. In Gaboriau's first crime story *L'Affaire Lerouge*, published in 1863,

A policeman on the beat in 1872

Lecoq is a minor character and a reformed criminal. As the stories continued he became the central character and his criminal past was dispensed with. Although the stories are sensational the police detective work and the workings of the French legal system are portrayed with realism and accuracy. Gaboriau's books were very popular outside France, and the extent of his fame can be judged by the fact that his most successful imitator outside France was a New Zealander, Fergus Hume. Hume's *The Mystery of a Hansom Cab* was a conscious attempt to emulate the success of Gaboriau's books, and it became the best selling novel of the nineteenth century. Unfortunately Hume did not benefit from this, for after publishing the book at his own expense in Australia in 1886, where it had some success, he came to England and was persuaded to sell the copyright for £50. Although Hume made a reasonable living as a writer and wrote over a hundred other books none of them achieved the same popularity.

The great popularity of this book, and the works of Gaboriau and Wilkie Collins, show to

16

An early library ticket

Emile Gaboriau

what an extent the public attitude to crime had changed during the nineteenth century. Romantic stories about criminals had given way to stories of detection; the detective, whether official or amateur, was no longer the corrupt bounty hunter of earlier times but a trusted protector of the innocent and defender of society.

The other significant social change had been the continuing increase in literacy. While novels were far too expensive for the working class their reading tastes had nevertheless become more sophisticated. The broad sheets of the early part of the century had given way to abridged novels and books that were published in weekly instalments. Lending libraries had also become more common, and although the intention had been to make books of an 'improving' nature available to the working class the demand for fiction was immediate and the libraries soon came to supply entertainment as well as education. The final step in the spread of literacy was the passing of the Education Act of 1870, whose aim was that all Britain should be able to read. The spread of rail travel also played a part in this process, for all but the smaller stations had bookstalls selling newspapers, magazines and cheap books. Books like *The Mystery of a Hansom Cab* achieved their huge sales partly in this way, but the most popular reading matter for the rail passengers became the magazine containing short stories.

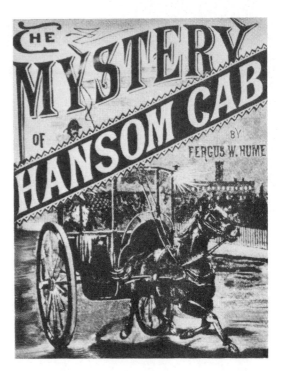

Conan Doyle's first two Sherlock Holmes stories are both full length novels, but they had only a modest success. It was not until he published his first short story in *The Strand* that he found real success.

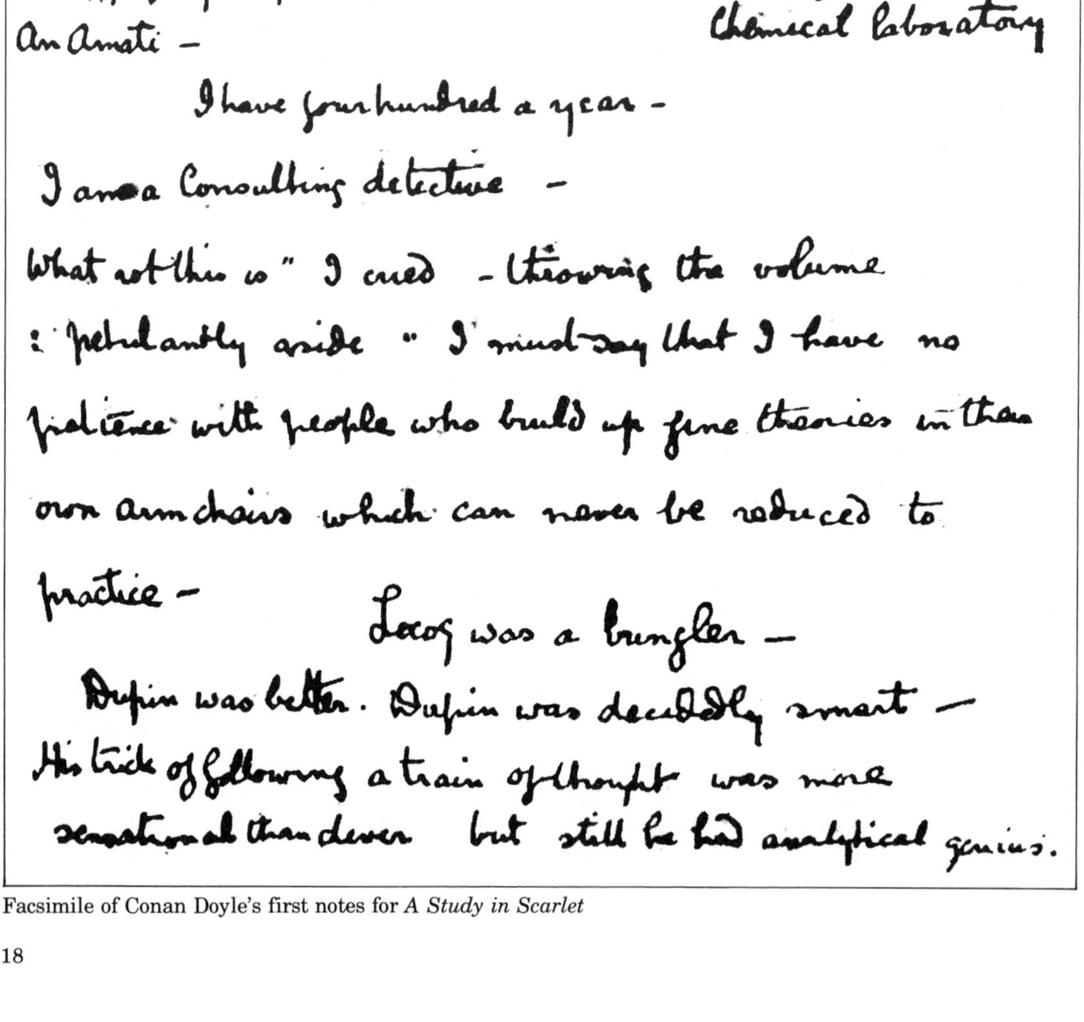

Study in Scarlet.

Ormond Sacker - from ~~Soudan~~ from Afghanistan
      Lived at 221 B Upper Baker Street
with

  J Sherrinford Holmes -

         The Laws of Evidence

  Reserved -
Sleepy eyed young man - philosopher - Collector of rare Violins
An Amati -   Chemical laboratory

    I have four hundred a year -

I am a Consulting detective -

What rot this is" I cried - throwing the volume
: petulantly aside " I must say that I have no
patience with people who build up fine theories in their
own armchairs which can never be reduced to
practice -
          Lecoq was a bungler -
  Dupin was better. Dupin was decidedly smart -
His trick of following a train of thought was more
sensational than clever but still he had analytical genius.

Facsimile of Conan Doyle's first notes for *A Study in Scarlet*

Dr Joseph Bell

About the origins of Holmes

CONAN DOYLE: *About the Sherlock Holmes stories. They came about in this way. I was quite a young doctor at the time. I had of course a scientific training, and I used occasionally to read detective stories. But it had always annoyed me how in the old-fashioned detective story the detective always seemed to get at his results either by some sort of lucky chance or fluke or else it was quite unexplained how he got there. He got there but he never gave an explanation how. That didn't seem to me quite playing the game. It seemed to me that he's bound to give his reasons why he came to his conclusions. Well, when I began to think about this, I began to think of turning scientific methods, as it were, on to the work of detection. And I used as a student to have an old professor – his name was Bell – who was extraordinarily quick at deductive work. He would look at the patient, he would hardly allow the patient to open his mouth, but he would make his diagnosis of the disease and also very often of the patient's nationality, and occupation and other points – entirely by his power of observation. So naturally I thought to myself – well, if a scientific man like Bell was to come into the detective business, he wouldn't do these things by chance, he'd get the thing by building it up scientifically.*

From a film interview included in the *Crime Writers* television series.

1
Holmes: The Hamlet of crime fiction

by Reginald Hill

So what's new about Sherlock Holmes?

Look at the stories and you don't find much that hasn't been done before, which is about as helpful as saying that there was a lot of sulphur, saltpetre and charcoal lying around before Friar Bacon invented gunpowder. On the other hand, look at what's been written about Holmes and you find analysis enough to daunt even the most enthusiastic hunter after truth. He is the Hamlet of crime fiction; everyone's tried to track him down and the ways are muddied by too many feet.

But even when we think we have him in our sights, he is no easy target. On the darkling plain of late Victorian literature he is a small peripheral figure; in the lost world of pure detective fiction, he looms like a mastodon; either way you can't be sure what you're aiming at.

Holmes to me has always been, first, Sydney Carton from *A Tale of Two Cities* and, second, an old teacher of mine, a sensitive, perceptive and sardonically witty man who is alive and well and possibly reading these words in amused disbelief. I make no attempt to explain or justify either impression, but they are what I come back to when I find the man himself becomes particularly elusive. Armed with these pictures, I shall try to track him down through the Victorian jungle. I shall distrust hearsay evidence, particularly Conan Doyle's. It is well known that authors when questioned about their purposes and their inspiration nearly always lie. And finally I shall look for him in places where there have been innumerable reported sightings almost as keenly as I shall look for him in places where there have been none.

If we agree that a fictional character is only as real as his publication dates, Sherlock Holmes was born in 1887, died in 1893, was resurrected, partially, in 1902 and wholly in 1905, took his last bow in 1917, and passed away in 1927. There are many thousands who would indignantly offer quite different and much more detailed biographies, but such accounts are religious rather than critical. They demonstrate the existence of a cult, they do not account for it. Holmes must be regarded as a creature of Conan Doyle's times, not of his own. He changes with those times, of course, but what he becomes when his renown is established is much less important than what it was that initially established that renown.

One thing that didn't happen was the kind of vast advance publicity campaign frequently used to sell books today. Even had the hard sell been possible in those less manipulative days Doyle would hardly have tolerated it. In 1897 he sharply and publicly rebuked a fellow writer, Hall Caine, for perpetrating advance 'puffs' of his novel *The Christian,* which, incidentally, sold 50,000 copies! Clearly the technique worked even then, but whatever it was that sold the Sherlock Holmes stories, it wasn't a campaign by his first British publisher who valued *A Study in Scarlet* at £25 – for the copyright! In fact, it took an American, J. M. Stoddart, editor of *Lippincott's Monthly Magazine* to spot the potential of Sherlock Holmes and commission a second story, *The Sign of Four.* Without Stoddart, Holmes might have sunk without trace.

A lunch which Stoddart gave in London produced the commission for Doyle and similarly benefited another writer of Irish descent, Oscar Wilde. Wilde's character and beliefs as expressed in the book he produced for Lippincott's – *The Picture of Dorian Gray,* seem diametrically opposed to all that Doyle wished to represent. The success of Holmes has more to do with the cheap, mass produced yellow-backs than the exotic Yellow Book, but at the same time the character of Holmes as described in *The Sign of Four* has a great deal of *fin de siècle* decadence about it. This languid, violin-playing, cocaine-addicted intellectual, expert on topics as remote and esoteric as Buddhism in Ceylon and medieval pottery, could have been one of Dorian Gray's own circle. Of course he is also revealed as an expert pugilist, not to mention a great detective, and by the mid-1890s (Holmes time), or ten years later (Doyle time), Watson has weaned him off the seven-percent solution of cocaine. Perhaps here we can see reflected public (i.e. middle class) opinion which has always known where to draw the line between what is pleasantly titillating and what is morally outrageous, and had drawn it pretty firmly mid-way through

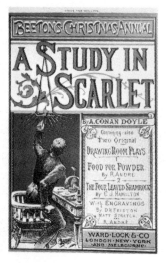

The cover of *Beeton's Christmas Annual* of 1887 in which Sherlock Holmes made his first appearance

Figures from the Decadent Movement – (*above*) Sargent's portrait of W. Graham Robertson, artist and author, and (*right*) J. E. Blanche's portrait of his fellow artist, Aubrey Beardsley

the nineties. What is certainly true is that throughout the books, from 1887 to 1927 (Doyle time), we find Holmes striking attitudes which would not jar too strongly with Lionel Johnson's advice to the would-be decadent in his essay 'The Cultured Faun' (1891).

'To play the part properly', Johnson tells us, 'a flavour of cynicism is recommended : a scientific profession of materialist dogmas, coupled – for you should forswear consistency – with gloomy chatter about 'The Will to Live' . . . Jumble all these 'impressions' together, your sympathies, your sorrows, your devotion and your despair; carry them about with you in a state of fermentation, and finally conclude that life is loathsome, yet that beauty is beatific.' Johnson could have provided his 'decadent' with a useful pocket-book of phrases culled from Holmes. 'My life is spent in one long effort to escape from the commonplaces of existence' (*The Red-Headed League*); 'What you do in this world is a matter of no consequence. The question is, what you can make people believe you have done' (*A Study in Scarlet*); 'Our highest assurance of the goodness of providence seems to me to rest in the flowers' (*The Naval Treaty*); 'What is the meaning of it, Watson? What object is served by this circle of misery and violence and fear?' (*The Cardboard Box*); 'Is not all life pathetic and futile?' . . . We reach. We grasp. And what is left in our hands at the end? A shadow. Or worse than a shadow – misery.' (*The Retired Colourman*).

"OUR VISITOR SPRANG FROM HIS CHAIR."

A Sidney Paget illustration to the Holmes story 'The Adventure of the Yellow Face'

Even his clothing ('he affected a certain quiet primness of dress') accords with Johnson's instruction ('externally our hero should cultivate a reassuring sobriety of habit'); and his physical appearance, tall, elegant, handsome, is that of a matinée idol, though of course it owes more to the illustrator Sidney Paget's use of his brother, Walter, as model than to Doyle's own descriptions.

I am not trying to suggest that these admittedly slight correspondences reflect any conscious intention on Doyle's part, but that they might possibly reflect the young writer's apprehension of his own age in which the decadent despair is but a *reductio ad absurdum* of the spiritual uncertainties which so often lay behind the thinking Victorian's material certainties. Doyle himself, brought up a Catholic, had soon lost his faith and spent a large part of his life looking for a substitute which he finally found in spiritualism.

Holmes, it seems to me, as he moves between the black pessimism of his contemplative moods and the energetic invigoration of his cases, has the makings of a representative hero of his times. His character is only sketched, of course, but there is sufficient detail suggested by the outline to capture the interest and exercise the imagination. The kind of hero that Doyle himself took (and wanted us to take) seriously was the kind of man shown in his historical stories – brave, courteous, faithful, patriotic. It is to Doyle's credit as an artist that he also made these men sometimes absurd and always human. But with Holmes he did something extra, almost by accident, or perhaps by neglect. He made him modern.

Holbrook Jackson, one of the first and finest chroniclers of the nineties, listed the period's main characteristics as 'the so-called decadence; the introduction of a sense of fact into literature and art; and the development of a transcendental view of social life.' Doyle hardly merits a mention by Jackson in *The Eighteen Nineties* and I would not quarrel with this. There are bigger fish to fry and Doyle's status is not at dispute, at least not by me. But I would suggest that such a success as the Sherlock Holmes stories had may owe something to considerations other than the more obvious and popular ones which we shall look at shortly.

Clearly the second of Holbrook Jackson's main characteristics is most obviously pertinent to Holmes. A sense of fact, both scientific and social, informs nearly all the stories, though it is I believe much less important than the sense of romance. But more of that later. The character of Holmes, I would claim, moves in the shadows of the 'so-called decadence', and this link with the dark side of Victorian dualism is reinforced through the dominant images of the stories (images dominant despite their actual rare appearance!) the fog, the dark, the reek of London, the ambiguous glow of gaslight, the foreign faces, the opium dens.

As for Holbrook Jackson's criterion, 'a transcendental view of social life', I make no large claims. Holmes however does quote Thoreau (in *The Noble Bachelor*) and has a great deal of that transcendentalist author's practical and artistic systematic application, which caused a contemporary to accuse him of watching nature 'like a detective who is to go upon the stand'. On the whole, though, Holmes is clearly even less of a transcendentalist than he is a decadent but in him the deductive and the intuitive processes sometimes overlap and blend in a peculiarly transcendental way, as when he says 'there is nothing in which deduction is so necessary as in religion' and offers as his argument the existence of a rose. Watson calls him 'an automaton – a calculating machine', but of course he is much more than that. Machines are not accessible upon the side of flattery, rarely have languid dreaming eyes, nor are they much subject to fits of black depression. Doyle set out to create a detective pure and simple, but his artistic instinct told him that a machine was not enough. Society's protectors must not stand apart from society. It is the process of detection which gives the stories their movement, but it is the character of Holmes that gives them their weight.

William Godwin

Shelley in his *Defence of Poetry* urged that as human knowledge increased one of the most important functions of the poet was to help us 'imagine what we know'. At the further end of the century writers like H. G. Wells and Jules Verne are certainly doing this with the monster, science, which had seemed a generation earlier to be a vast and perilous threat to romantic notions of beauty. And in a small way Doyle in the Sherlock Holmes stories is similarly overcoming another old enemy of romantic art, the human reason.

If Shelley seems to have made a rather sudden entrance at this point, it's not without purpose. To understand the kind of literature that Conan Doyle was to have such an influence on, it's useful to know something of its origins, and *Caleb Williams,* the book which is often nowadays regarded as the first detective novel, was written by Shelley's father-in-law, William Godwin. But the relationship was more than just the accidental one of marriage. Godwin was a rationalist

Conan Doyle in later years

philosopher who taught that institutionalised society was the major obstacle to the perfection of man through reason. His teachings had a large influence on Shelley and others of the major romantic writers and thus on the whole course of romanticism in the English speaking world. His connection with the detective story is therefore twofold; first as the author of something which in content is more like a detective novel than anything written before, and in manner of composition, (that is, the climax and denouement being conceived before the story which leads up to them), is precisely like a detective novel; secondly, and more importantly, as a formative influence on the greatest names of that movement to which the detective story undeniably belongs. For let it here be clearly understood, if my hints have not been taken already, that the Sherlock Holmes stories and indeed all of detective fiction, whatever it may claim of science and reason, belong to *romantic* literature. Confusingly the term *classical* is sometimes applied to detective stories of the so-called 'Golden Age' to indicate that they comply with certain conventions. But these conventions are simply practical limitations and in no way related to a philosophical concept of life as are the main conventions of classical art. Conan Doyle when he said farewell to his Holmes stories in 1927 made no distinction of kind (though elsewhere he made a great distinction of quality) between them and his much-loved historical novels, only hoping that their readers might have experienced 'that distraction from the worries of life and stimulating change of thought which can only be found in the fairy kingdom of romance'.

It is, of course, no coincidence that this particular function of romantic literature and the audience that required it should have evolved at the same time. Q. D. Leavis in her book *Fiction and the Reading Public* writes, 'it is generally recognised that the universal need to read something when not actively employed has been created by the conditions of modern life'. And by 'modern life' is meant urban industrial life whose beginnings (if such a monstrous growth can be said to have beginnings) are coincident with and in many ways causal of that shift of feeling and cultural emphasis we call the Romantic Revival.

These are matters too complex for discussion here, as is Mrs Leavis's ambiguous assertion that 'the old order made reading to prevent boredom unnecessary'. What cannot be contested, however, is the fact that during the nineteenth century an ever growing body of readers among the lower middle and working classes were revealing appetites for reading matter which no-one was yet properly equipped to supply. Parliament interested itself in the problem and typical among the evidence supplied is the following. J. W. Day, Chairman of Houghton-le-Spring Poor Law Union wrote in 1842, 'in winter they have no mode of employing their vacant time, and they spend it unprofitably . . . the few who have had a little education are fond of reading, but they are mostly without the means of obtaining books'.

Seven years later, writing to a Select Committee on Public Libraries, Samuel Smiles repeated the plea and added to it the assertion that many people who had learned to read and write as young children had practically forgotten how for want of opportunity to practice, a claim which was still being made from the floor of the House in 1855. Richard Altick in *The English Common Reader* warns against Victorian literacy statistics and when we see that between 1841 and 1900 the male literacy rate is alleged by official figures to have risen from 67.3 per cent to 97.2 per cent, we can understand why. The size of the final figure is hardly believable and presumably the size of the earlier one is also exaggerated (by the method of assessment, not by government dishonesty of course); but there is no reason to question the *proportion* of the increase, and this is vast enough. The proof of the market must lie in the demand and the way in which the sale of periodicals and newspapers expanded during the second half of the century is proof enough. Not surprisingly, the greatest expansion tended

Paget illustration for 'The Adventure of the Cardboard Box'

W. H. Smith railway bookstall about the turn of the century

to be at the lower end of the market and the great critical reviews which had dominated intellectual life at the beginning of the century benefited little from the reading explosion. Writing in *Household Words* in 1858, Wilkie Collins (the author of *The Moonstone*, the first and perhaps the greatest *real* detective novel) said of these 'new' readers, 'the future of English fiction may rest with this unknown public which is now waiting to be taught the difference between a good book and a bad. . . . To the penny journals of the present time belongs the credit of having discovered a new public.'

That the 'new public' had been discovered was certainly true. Whether it has ever been taught the difference between a good book and a bad is doubtful. Not that in the Victorian era there was a shortage of these willing to try. But there was also no shortage of those who greeted the new public with a fervour which was commercial rather than educational. Industry was not slow to discover ways to satisfy the need it had helped to create. Cheaper techniques of paper manufacture were evolved, paper duty was repealed, technology made illustration easy and inexpensive, new high-speed mechanical presses were designed. And all these were used to feed the rapacious mouth of perhaps the most famous offspring of that nineteenth century marriage between Art and Industry, the railway station bookstall. W. H. Smith obtained the monopoly in the 1840's and cheap editions of novels for this new and growing market of travelling readers soon abounded, including the famous yellow-backs, so called after the colour of their glossy binding. Full-length novels were now available in a format and at a price which put them within reach of nearly all of the new mass reading public. And the continuation of serial publication in magazines and weekly newspapers put the work of most of the period's best novelists into the hands of the rest.

The tradition of serial publication began effectively with Dickens' *Pickwick Papers* in 1836 when its purpose was, in part, to get round the extremely high volume price of books. By 1890 when George Newnes founded *The Strand,* the magazine with which he hoped to mop up the middle ground between the readers of his *Tit-Bits* (1880) and the disciples of the intellectual reviews, serialisation was no longer in total cost a cheap alternative to volume purchase. It was principally a circulation boosting element in a magazine or newspaper.

The Strand was very much a 'modern' magazine. It was full of photographs, offered a 'free gift' (a print of a painting in the Royal Academy) and featured interviews with celebrities, as well as general articles and, of course, fiction. It rapidly built up a readership of over 300,000. Conan Doyle in 1891 had had short stories published before, in magazines like *The Cornhill, Temple Bar, London Society,* and *Cassell's Saturday Journal.* They had not gone unremarked but the short story rarely has a long life. In addition, *A Study in Scarlet* and *The Sign of Four* had appeared but with hardly more splash than his short

Two covers for
The Strand Magazine

Paget's drawing of
Holmes' arch-enemy,
Professor Moriarty

stories. Only the reception of his historical novel, *Micah Clarke,* had given him much encouragement.

What he now offered *The Strand* was something relatively new – a series of self-contained episodes from the life of one central character, thus combining the instant attraction of the short story with the accumulative attraction of the serial.

What *The Strand* offered Doyle was completely new to him. An instant readership of 300,000 plus!

Whether another Sherlock Holmes novel, or indeed the twelve stories of *The Adventures* could have reached anything like such a public in volume form is extremely doubtful. Perhaps their success would have been just as great, though certainly delayed. I do not think so. I think it is one of the happier coincidences of literary history that *The Strand* provided Doyle at the same time with an audience and, just as important, with an impetus to present Holmes in that short form which was to show him off to his very best advantage.

The trouble with explanations is finding one that explains everything simply and clearly. I have tried to place Holmes in the widest context of literature, both in his own times and in the greater movement to which the stories belong. The only thing I have not yet explained is why, when Holmes finally met his public, he was greeted with the fearful enthusiasm usually reserved for messiahs!

Doyle was astounded and ultimately disconcerted by his success. And nowhere does he himself offer any cogent explanation of it. It's possible, if he had sat down in the late 1880s and made a projection from the known facts as he did with regard to the potential threat of German U-boats in 1917, that he might have arrived at Holmes by a technique almost Holmesian. But he didn't. We, however, need not play at Holmes. We can simply use the method devised by Godwin and followed by all detective fiction writers thereafter (not to mention all historians since the world began); that is, working back from a known conclusion and seeing how best to arrange the events that precede it.

A society without an effective police force tries to protect itself by the threat of disproportionately harsh punishment. So-called hardliners still manifest the syndrome today. This was the situation in Britain during the eighteenth century, whence the names which survive to us from the great game of law and order are invariably criminals – Turpin, Wild, MacHeath etc. But you cannot have a fast-growing, property-

owning and indeed novel-reading middle class without a
growing demand for protection. The biggest threat to criminals is always detection and therefore it's not surprising that
those people who most desire the protection should support
whatever detective myths arise about their protectors.

Such a myth clothed the often dubious activities of the Bow
Street Horse and Foot Patrol at the start of the nineteenth
century and it's interesting to note that when Dickens lends
his weight to the new myth of the Detective Police (established
1842) in an article in *Household Words* in 1850, he opens with
a paragraph debunking the Bow Streeters. Overlapping myths
may not co-exist. Holmes for the most part is blessed with a
gang of dull plodders at Scotland Yard and elsewhere. When
he finally meets with a man he can admire, Inspector Baynes
of the Surrey Constabulary, the union is uneasy, the work
duplicated and Holmes (dare we say it?) superfluous. This
battle between the amateur and the professional – or the
unofficial and the offical – is constant throughout detective
fiction both between writers and within books. Dickens,
Collins and Gaboriau throw their considerable weight down on
the side of the official, but there is a danger here. In real terms,
the police force obviously are much more credible, but the very
weight of their reality can be a disadvantage.

Myths exist on the whole to confirm the possibility of order
in the chaos of life. Society, we plainly see, is chaotic. The
police force is an institution of society and therefore suspect.
For most of the time we prefer to maintain the myth of the
bumbling hardly competent bobby, which enables us to order
our fear of an overpowerful police (a fear expressed by
eighteenth-century social philosophers such as Blackstone
and Paley, and echoed by a parliamentary committee chaired
by Robert Peel in 1822). Even Dickens in his *Household Words*
article which gives a highly laudatory account of an interview
with the new detective force, cannot resist ending by telling us
gleefully that one of them had his pocket picked on the way
home.

But let us be clear. Without a police force there can be no
detective fiction, though several modern writers have, with
varying degrees of success, tried to write detective stories set
in pre-police days. Doyle was born into policed society, a
society which fifty years earlier had made the decision that the
growth of crime was a greater threat to its liberties than the
growth of a police force. But the point was still debatable and,
worse, the efficiency of that force was not yet proven. Jack the
Ripper was never taken up and no less a person than the Queen
expressed the fear that the Detective Department was not as

Contemporary illustration of
the discovery of one of the
victims of Jack the Ripper

efficient as it might be. *Punch* referred to it with typical
subtlety as the 'defective department'.

Within this society which admired, mocked, relied on and
distrusted its police, the interest in crime had never been
greater. When Watson, upon very short acquaintance, makes
out a list of Holmes's 'limits' in *A Study in Scarlet,* item 9
reads, 'knowledge of sensational literature – immense. He
appears to know every detail of every horror perpetrated in the
century.' This is a fund of knowledge he must have shared with
many tens of thousands who would have matched him also on
item 1 of Watson's list, 'knowledge of literature – nil'. Presumably by 'sensational literature' Watson means those
accounts of real-life events which were snapped up so avidly by
the semi-literate masses throughout the century.

Holmes obviously fed all this interesting reading into his
computer-like mind and drew upon it when necessary. We find
him saying in *The Red-Headed League,* 'As a rule when I hear
some slight indication of the course of events, I am able to
guide myself by the thousands of other similar cases which
occur to my memory.'

Clearly the motives for his study are of the purest, but the
generality of readers were spurred by other more cloudy
desires. The twentieth century may claim to have discovered
the pornography of violence, but the nineteenth was getting a
very large kick out of crime long before Jules Verne had
invented television.

Nor was the taste for the sensational limited to any single group of society then, any more than it is now. Only the sources changed, and though the Sherlock Holmes stories were certainly far removed from what Watson intended to be understood as 'sensational literature', they were almost as far removed (in Doyle's eyes, at least) from what the Doctor categorised as 'literature'. There is a very strong sensational element in many of the stories; a message scribbled in blood, a head blown apart by a shotgun; a hanged man's neck drawn out like a plucked chicken's; two newly-severed ears in a cardboard box; the examples are endless. And the stories that contain them are presented as *cases* of Sherlock Holmes to a public most of whom are familiar by one means or another with a whole gallery of what they know to be real-life crimes reported in even more sensational detail. A novel involves by its length, but usually feels like fiction, especially in serial form. But these stories, short, sharp, convincingly written, with just enough of background material from Watson as such a conscientious chronicler might be expected to give, found an audience ready to be persuaded that they *might* be true and, in many cases, easily persuaded that they were.

To sum up then. There was an audience waiting and *The Strand Magazine* marshalled it. It wanted sensation. It wanted authenticity. It wanted reassurance. Doyle's skill as a scene painter gave them the first. His choice of form gave them the second. And his creation of an amateur scientific detective gave them the third. For a police detective such as the English reader was familiar with in the person of Dickens' Inspector Bucket or Collins' Sergeant Cuff or Gaboriau's translated Lecoq ('a miserable bungler') could not be a scientist, nor a graduate, nor a gentleman, and what stood behind him was a suspect institution, not an abstract concept of justice. Sherlock Holmes satisfied all the market requirements. He was an advertising agency's dream. He was to become his creator's nightmare.

But having said all this, is it yet enough to explain the phenomenon of Holmes? Not quite; an element must be missing. For Holmes continues to delight long after the circumstances of his creation have become as dull as academic history.

Doyle's most obvious literary debt was to Poe who in four or five stories published forty years earlier had laid down blueprints for the form which are still followed to this day.

William Gillette

(Interestingly, for it takes us back to my starting point, Poe's other major sphere of influence was, via Baudelaire, on the symbolist movement of the 90s which had strong links with the 'so-called decadence'.) Three of Poe's detective stories, or 'tales of ratiocination' as he preferred to call them, feature Dupin, his gifted amateur detective who reaches his conclusions by pure reasoning, is wayward and moody, prefers night to day, has a faithful if rather dumb friend who acts as his chronicler, and cooperates wearily with the inefficient official police. Doyle acknowledged his debt happily and openly, though there was a certain subtlety in making Holmes himself refer to the Poe stories, thus reducing them firmly to fiction and, by implication, bringing his own casebook nearer fact. But superficially the resemblance is so close that it's probably worthwhile glancing at the differences to make sure nothing has been omitted in this attempt to account for Sherlock Holmes.

Poe apparently held his 'tales of ratiocination' in as low esteem as Doyle did Holmes. 'Where' he asks 'is the ingenuity of unravelling a web which you (the author) have woven for the express purpose of unravelling?' The answer of course is that the ingenuity lies in the weaving. Doyle weaves more than just a web, he weaves a tapestry which has in it characters and

Holmes and Watson travel to Dartmoor to solve the mystery of 'Silver Blaze'

Three film portrayals of Sherlock Holmes and Doctor Watson. (Top opposite) Eille Norwood and Hubert Willis in 1922; (*below opposite*) Basil Rathbone and Nigel Bruce in 1939; (*right*) Peter Cushing and André Morell in 1959

relationships, scenes and seasons, as well as the threads of a puzzle.

Holmes inhabits a London which his creator remembers from boyhood visits and adult habitation. Dupin inhabits a Paris his creator never saw. Think of Holmes and you get a picture; think of Dupin and you have to think twice to make sure you are not thinking of Arsène Lupin, and you can't remember what he looks like either. In the Holmes stories, the puzzle is always important but it rarely completely dominates. In the Dupin stories, the puzzle is all. And yet Poe allows flaws of reasoning to appear, more glaring because more central than anything we get from Doyle. Both became involved in real cases. Poe 'fictionalised' the death of a New York girl, Mary Rogers, under the title 'The Mystery of Marie Roget'. His sole purpose seems to have been to demonstrate the virtues of his new ratiocinative techniques, and he claimed (with little justice) to have solved the mystery. Doyle on the other hand got involved in his most important real cases, those of George Edalji and of Oscar Slater, because he felt an important question of justice was involved. In both cases he was largely instrumental in having a wrongful verdict overthrown though not without the expense of considerable amounts of time and of money. In both cases (and in several of the numerous others which a hopeful public were forever tossing at 'Sherlock Holmes') he applied the kind of deductive reasoning he makes Holmes use, and it worked.

But it's not just a matter of alleging that Doyle had a better grasp of the method than Poe. The important thing is that the desire for truth and justice which was so strong in Doyle himself is communicated to his creation and informs all that the great detective undertakes. The new dimension which Holmes brought to detective fiction is quite simply depth. He is an absurd and outrageous figure, but his absurdities are for the most part relatable to the age in which he lives, unlike some of his so-called successors of the 'Golden Age' who are vacuities inhabiting vacuums. Some of his predecessors, notably Bucket and Cuff, appear in books which might appear to have more claim to 'depth' than any of the Holmes stories. But these detectives are only part, and a far from central part, of those novels. Holmes is ninety per cent, and in any case when we think of him we do not think of a single story, but the whole vast saga.

Some critics invite us to marvel at the way in which Holmes anticipated many investigatory techniques later to become normal CID practice. That's interesting but hardly important. After all, the early readers didn't know he was anticipating and the later ones (unless they read the critics) aren't aware that he did so! What is both interesting *and* important is that by his synthesis of the scientific temper of the Victorian Age and the old heroic myth of good and evil, law and order, Doyle offers us something of a 'criticism of life' in the Holmes stories.

Perhaps here is where he blunted the sharp creative edge that might have carved out of history the significant novels he intended his romances to be. They are exciting and colourful but there is something merely absurd about the pursuit of knightly honour when set alongside Holmes' simple claim that he has left London (that is to say, the world) a better place. 'I am not aware that I have ever used my powers on the wrong side.'

Surely this is the authentic heroic voice, and here at last perhaps is the real secret of Holmes. 'Golden Ages' give birth to mere empty pastorals, while the child of the true heroic age is the epic. And the epic proper, as every schoolboy once knew, is a parcel of exciting stories about a great but human hero sung to the people by a melodious bard. The critics and the conventions are just loutish latecomers who may disturb but must not distract the listeners.

Doyle is the bard. Holmes is his hero. The listening seems likely to go on for ever.

Further Reading

There's a great deal of fairly quirky stuff available on Holmes, of interest mainly to confirmed Sherlockians. If you are one you will know it. If not, I see no reason to encourage you. There is no harm, however, in browsing through an entertaining companion volume such as Michael and Molly Hardwick's *The Sherlock Holmes Companion* (John Murray, 1962). What is really interesting and useful, I think, is to see the Holmes stories against the total background of Conan Doyle's fascinating and eventful life. There are several biographies to chose from. The three below are all in their differing ways very readable.

Hesketh Pearson: *Conan Doyle his life and art* (Methuen, 1943; White Lion Pubs., 1974; Macdonald and Jane's, 1977)

John Dickson Carr: *The Life of Sir Arthur Conan Doyle* (John Murray, 1949)

Charles Higham: *The Adventures of Conan Doyle* (Hamish Hamilton, 1976)

Anyone interested in the growth of the mass reading public which made possible the kind of publishing we are familiar with in the twentieth century will find the following full of fascination:

Q. D. Leavis: *Fiction and the Reading Public* (Chatto, 1932)

Richard D. Altick: *The English Common Reader: a social history of the mass reading public, 1800–1900* (University of Chicago Press, 1957)

Finally after you have finished all the Holmes stories, try those of his contemporaries. After Holmes, the floodgates opened and a great number of strange but sometimes extremely tasty fish came pouring through.

Many of the best have been collected and introduced by Hugh Greene in three volumes: *The Rivals of Sherlock Holmes: early detective stories* (Bodley Head, 1971; Penguin Books, 1971); *More Rivals of Sherlock Holmes: cosmopolitan crimes* (Bodley Head, 1971; Penguin Books, 1973); *Crooked Counties: further rivals* . . . (Bodley Head, 1973; Penguin Books, 1975).

After Holmes

The enormous success of the Sherlock Holmes stories sparked off a whole host of imitations and variants. There were supermen, like Jacques Futrelle's 'Thinking Machine', Professor S. F. X. Van Dusen, who solved his cases by reason alone, Ernest Bramah's blind detective Max Carrados, and Baroness Orczy's Old Man in the Corner who, without moving from his seat in an ABC tea-room solved cases that had been baffling the police. These and the others from the same mould all have their Watson figure to act as a foil for their brilliance. Bramah's Max Carrados and his assistant, Louis Carlyle, are a particularly satisfying combination, as Carrados' blindness provides a sound reason for the relationship between them, and also gives more scope for the development of Carlyle's character. R. Austin Freeman gave his detective Dr Thorndyke an extremely calm and rational attitude to his cases. He is a forensic scientist working clearly and logically (and often with the aid of Freeman's medical knowledge) but he is so unemotional that he has almost no personality and his narrator companion, Dr Jervis, has no chance at all to become a character.

R. Austin Freeman and his creation Dr Thorndyke

Other writers avoided the superman image for their detectives and made them ordinary men, often private investigators. This ordinary man usually works alone as he needs no Watson to shine against. Arthur Morrison's Martin Hewitt stories, which first appeared in *The Strand* in 1894, were a reaction to the Holmesian superman. Hewitt was physically different – stout, average height and round faced – and he relied entirely on ordinary abilities and common sense to solve his cases. There were other stories with ordinary men as detectives, like the Paul Beck stories by M. McDonnell Bodkin, but the superman detective was the dominant character in the short stories of the time.

The superman did have considerable advantages for the writers, for although he often led to difficulties with characterization he was much better at investigating plots that might baffle the ordinary reader and yet be logical.

Two television
portrayals of Raffles
and his friend,
Bunny.
(*Above*) Anthony Valentine
and Christopher Strauli;
(*below*) Jeremy Clyde
and Michael Cochrane
from the *Crime Writers*
programmes

Running counter to the main body of writing, which favoured law and order, are the Raffles stories written by E. W. Hornung. Hornung was Conan Doyle's brother-in-law, and Doyle disapproved of the idea of a criminal as hero. A. J. Raffles, the gentleman burglar, and his accomplice, Bunny, are almost the negative image of Holmes and Watson, reversing both their temperament and moral attitude. Behind the facade of a perfect English gentleman Raffles is a burglar stealing simply to keep himself in the style to which he feels entitled. Raffles' excellence as an amateur cricketer is used in some of the stories to underline his strict adherence to social conventions in everything but theft. He is a long way from the eighteenth-century criminal hero at war with society. Raffles steals to keep his place in society.

Film versions of Raffles. (*Opposite*) Ronald Colman in 1930; (*right*) David Niven in 1940

The other successful criminal hero of the time was Arsène Lupin in the stories written by Maurice Leblanc. Like Raffles, Lupin is ultimately on the side of society and not a rebel, and in some of the stories he almost plays the role of a detective. In spite of the success of the Raffles and Lupin stories, the criminal hero could not withstand the weakening of his character that this degree of conformity demanded, and did not appear again for many years.

Standing slightly apart from the other creations of the period is G. K. Chesterton's Father Brown. This dumpy, untidy and apparently ordinary little priest with his flapping umbrella and brown paper parcels is unique amongst fictional detectives. Although he is not one of the supermen of detection he is certainly not an ordinary man. His solutions to crimes are often arrived at by theological reasoning or moral observation. Chesterton was an exuberant and witty writer, and although he was the first president of the Detection Club, the body founded for detective-story writers, he never felt himself constrained by its rules about what should or should not make a good detective story. The Father Brown stories exist on their own terms, and within these the clues work and the solutions are fair.

813 A NEW ARSÈNE LUPIN ADVENTURE BY MAURICE LEBLANC

MILLS & BOON L^{TD}   LONDON

45

(*Left*) G. K. Chesterton towards the end of his life. (*Bottom left*) Alec Guinness as Father Brown in the 1954 film; (*below*) Kenneth More as the television Father Brown in 1973

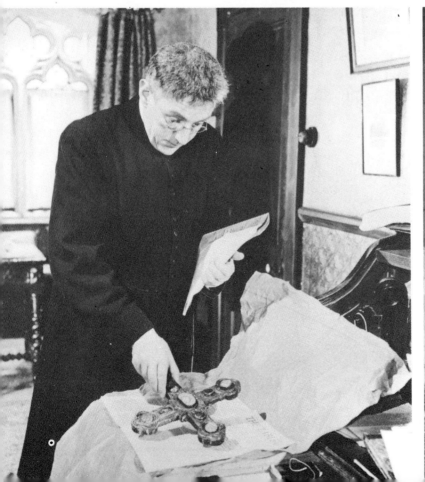

It is characteristic of Chesterton's skill and humanity that while many of his stories are in effect moral lessons this never once interferes with our enjoyment of the story for its own sake. The wit, the love of paradox and the delight in language, these things, together with Chesterton's morality and concern for humanity put his stories in a separate category.

The short story was the dominant form until after the first world war, but the novel did not disappear. A. E. W. Mason wrote several books featuring Inspector Hanaud of the Sûreté and his friend Mr Ricardo. They appear for the first time in *At the Villa Rose* published in 1910, but not again until after the first world war in *The House of the Arrow* (1924), and *The Prisoner in the Opal* (1928). Mason was not primarily a writer of crime stories, but a successful author of historical romances. He bought much from his other writing to his crime stories and they are a good deal more atmospheric than those of many of his contemporaries.

A.E.W.Mason

In 1913 E. C. Bentley published *Trent's Last Case*. The book was conceived as a humorous demolition of the omniscient detective. Trent works hard to discover the solution to the mystery, and his piecing together of the clues is convincingly done, but at the end we discover that he is completely wrong. The book was a great success, and was regarded as something new in detective stories, but it was centred too strongly on the single joke of the investigator's

mistaken solution to lead to any further development. It was not until the twenties that this humorous approach to the detective story reappeared, particularly in the books of Monsignor Ronald Knox.

Monsignor Ronald Knox

Mrs Belloc Lowndes is best remembered for her novel *The Lodger,* also published in 1913. It is a fictitious account of the events surrounding Jack the Ripper, the killer who had terrified London only twenty-five years previously.

Although these and other novels were popular it was not until the twenties that the short story lost its dominant position and the novel came into favour. This change in reading habits was accelerated by the rise of the lending libraries. Boot's, the chemists, and W. H. Smith's, the book and newspaper sellers, were nationwide organisations with outlets in most towns and cities, but as well as them many small newsagents and bookshops ran their own libraries lending books for a few pennies a week or in return for an annual subscription.

The new taste in reading matter reflected the changes that had taken place in society. The emancipation of women and the expansion of the middle class meant that there was now a new and sizable readership – the middle-class housewife. The writers too had changed in a corresponding way. The twenties saw the emergence of many women writers, and they played a leading part in what has been called the 'Golden Age' of the detective story, the nineteen twenties and thirties.

2
Mayhem Parva and Wicked Belgravia

by Colin Watson

The habits of people, their ways of thought, their ambitions and prejudices, all may be divined more clearly from a reading of their favourite books than from the theses of the historian and the sociologist.

A particularly rich seam of this kind of information is the detective fiction of the years between the two world wars. From Edgar Wallace to Leslie Charteris, from Mrs Belloc Lowndes to Agatha Christie, from Freeman Wills Crofts to Margery Allingham, the providers of entertainment by crime puzzle were contributing – often unwittingly – clues to a much more intriguing mystery: that of the behaviour and beliefs of the British middle class in the 1920s and 1930s.

Those two decades came to be known as the Golden Age of the detective story, but the epithet might mislead. There was, for instance, no sudden flowering of literary talent that was likely to outlast its generation, although a number of competent professionals did become established. Nor was there created a public demand for crime fiction comparable with that which absorbed the massive prints of the post-war years. Agatha Christie's sales in hardback ranged between three and five thousand, long after newspapers had come to refer to her as a 'famous' author, and none of her novels sold as many as ten thousand in its first year until 1935, when *Three Act Tragedy* was published.

What did distinguish the so-called Golden Age was the formation of a habit, the establishment of a convention. The detective story had come to be accepted as an interesting fact of

life – even by the thousands who had never read one. Words such as 'tec, clue, fingerprint, blunt instrument, were used with a familiarity, and often with an affectionate facetiousness, that indicated universal recognition of what the whodunnit was about.

No one called Watson, whose childhood coincided with the period, is likely to forget the maddening frequency with which he encountered the fatuous misquotation 'Elementary, my dear Watson' at school. And yet, what proportion of those who were so prompt with references to the creations of Conan Doyle could claim to have worked their way through even a part of the Sherlock Holmes stories?

Doyle wrote for the class who took *The Strand Magazine* and to which he himself belonged, the British middle class. His readers were clerks, shopkeepers, professional men, travellers on suburban railway lines, colonisers of the new estates that rail had opened up. They would have seen nothing strange in Doyle's presentation of working men, of the areas they frequented, of the types of criminal recruited from their ranks. These characters, to an even greater degree than the dukes, landowners, and international diplomats portrayed as clients of Holmes, are distanced by the author's own social segregation: when he refers to a countryman as a 'peasant', as he does more than once, he is not being gratuitously arrogant; the labourer really is as remote from Doyle's experience as if he had come out of another age or country.

It did not matter in the least that this gap existed. The story was everything, the working out of the puzzle, the entertainment.

And spreading out from the keen, but still restricted, enjoyment of crime fiction, as Doyle and his imitators and immediate successors conceived it, was a myth – ultimately to become universal – the myth of the Detective, or Morality Reasserted by Deduction.

Early crime stories had been simply melodrama in print, embodying the declamatory phraseology of the barn-stormer theatrical companies, with lots of 'horrids' and 'dreadfuls'. The language of the shilling shocker doubtless was evolved in the first place as a means of gaining attention by frightening people. Until less than half a century ago, newspaper reporting, too, commonly employed the same technique. Every murder was liable to be dubbed 'foul' or 'brutal' or 'horrible' – as if to distinguish it from a fair, or elegant, killing, or perhaps one occasioned by good-natured caprice.

Conan Doyle was faithful to the same tradition. He saw no reason to put the description of crime into urbane terms. In the

Holmes stories, a blow is forthrightly declared to have been 'frightful' and its victim 'unfortunate'. The bicycle in 'The Adventure of the Priory School' is 'horribly' smeared with blood, while a witness has 'a face with horror in every lineament'. The duke of the same story, his duplicity discovered, turns not white, but 'ghastly white'.

The use of so heavy-handed a technique, even by writers capable of remarkable subtlety, emphasises the uncomplicated assumptions regarding good and evil that the reading public shared with their favourite authors in Victorian times and for some years of the new century. It might be asked if the assumptions survived the first world war and whether the detective story writers of the Golden Age displayed a less naïve attitude towards their growing readership.

At first sight, it could appear that during the 1920s and 1930s the raw elements of melodrama did give place to more sophisticated themes and treatment. The pitch, certainly, changed radically. Any detective who, after the first world war, plucked off a disguise and announced his identity in the ringing tones of an Irving, would have stood little chance of repeat appearances. The police themselves, who had been presented as often as not by Victorian crime writers, including Dickens and Wilkie Collins, as romantic tough-nuts on the models of the old thief-takers and Bow Street Runners, were now becoming institution men, more or less credible, some clever, some stupid, but all identifiable with a safe, solid and satisfactory social system.

Another change was in the type of crime. The old writers seem to have been assured of gasps of outrage at the drop of a family heirloom into a thief's pocket. The stealing of jewels had been a theme sufficient to sustain interest in a novel of several hundred pages. So had the loss, or threatened loss, of a reputation, particularly that of a titled person or a statesman. Now, in the paradoxically more cosy and homely atmosphere favoured by the Golden Age authors, murder was a minimum requirement, even for a short story.

Much broader qualifications for the role of criminal were implicit in the new style. He did not need to be a spy or a foreigner or a dispossessed claimant to a throne or a fortune. Beasts in human form were, in general, out. Uncontrollable rages and faces in which was discernible pure evil had had their day, though they did linger on, noticeably in the pages of the 'thriller' writers (e.g. Horler, Sapper, Wheatley, etc.) as distinct from the detection school. Indeed, growing emphasis upon the mystery element had led quite early in the period to a real difficulty: how to present as a normal, even likeable,

person for 199 pages, someone who was to be unmasked as a murderer on page 200.

Was this, then, realism? Were the readers being shown, for the first time through the pages of a kind of book formerly unashamedly fantastic and escapist, a picture of life as it was lived, a portrait of their times?

Not according to Raymond Chandler, the gifted American who had brought an English education and wit to the service of his native perception in writing a handful of the best crime novels of the century. Of Agatha Christie, Dorothy L. Sayers and their fellow practitioners, he declared that:

the only reality the English detection writers knew was the conversational accent of Surbiton and Bognor Regis.

The following is what, in his essay, 'The Simple Art of Murder', Chandler wrote of Sayers in particular, but the criticism is just as valid in a general application:

Her kind of detective story was an arid formula which could not even satisfy its own implications. It was second-grade literature because it was not about the things that could make first-grade literature. If it started out to be about real people . . . they must very soon do unreal things in order to form the artificial pattern required by the plot. When they did unreal things, they ceased to be real themselves. They became puppets and cardboard lovers and papier-mâché villains and detectives of exquisite and impossible gentility.

The judgment may be felt today to be unreasonably devoid of allowances – Chandler was, after all, writing of people whose prime role was to entertain – but it is not inaccurate. In book after book of the inter-war years they duly appeared – the decent, self-deprecatory chaps in tennis togs; the plucky girls of good complexion and propensity for getting locked in cellars with homicidal companions; the frail old ladies with small private incomes who spend all their time tending the garden and noticing enormously significant facts about comings and goings; the dowdy companions with grudges, and their unlovable employers, forever cutting someone or other out of their wills; the aristocrats concealing forensic omniscience beneath a veneer of asininity; the assortments of house-party guests, forever dressing for dinner and hunting missing daggers; and, of course, the ubiquitous butlers, chauffeurs, housemaids and other lower orders, all comic, surly or sinister, but none quite human.

Theirs was a world that was self-contained and never changing. One flat in Half Moon Street was exactly like another. The same Tudor mansion, half-an-hour's Bentley ride from town, might have served for all the stories, so long as it

(*Opposite*)
Agatha Christie in 1946

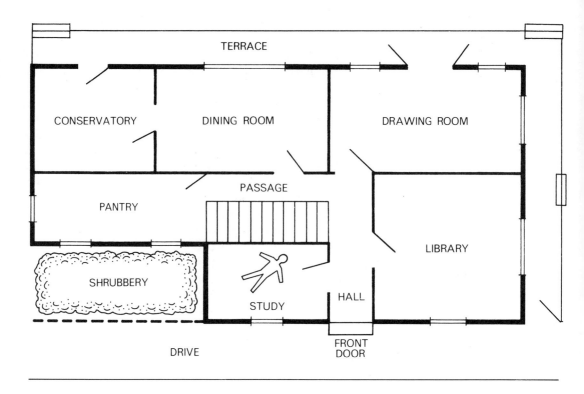

possessed a library and a study (veritable abattoirs, those studies) and french windows opening upon a lawn, and lockable bedrooms.

Most of the characters were of independent means. These ranged from modest pensions to inherited wealth and, naturally, were often strongly related to motive. What was important was to ensure that suspects had leisure for crime; a nine-to-five job was so hard to reconcile with the elaborate time-table on which the plot commonly depended that the working man or woman could not be accommodated without a great deal of trouble.

Another necessary ingredient of the Golden Age mystery novel was the observance of convention, as it was then understood. The expected unexpectedness of the criminal's identity, its well-I-never-ness, so to speak, depended upon a certain uniformity of behaviour within the circle of characters. Caddishness, one could be sure, was but a red herring. If there was any church-going to be done, it was ten to one that the criminal would be one of the congregation. *Outré* opinions, eccentric political views, and offensive artistic affectations – all these were fingerposts in the opposite direction from guilt. An especially interesting aspect of this way of misleading readers in accordance with their own wishes is its clear indication of the sort of thing which was likely to irritate respectable people forty or fifty years ago.

Perhaps the most sensitive area of intolerance was that of racial difference. The old-style thrillers had long been packed with despicable and evil-intentioned foreigners, and the writers of the more sedate detective stories saw no reason why they should not devote part of their talent to splenetic portraiture of characters with dark complexions or funny accents. Foreign had been synonymous with criminal in nine books out of ten, and the conclusion is inescapable that as big a proportion of readers found the notion perfectly reasonable.

There was now one concession to sophistication. References to ethnic origin were no longer framed with the crudity so obviously enjoyed by Sax Rohmer and 'Sapper' and E. W. Hornung. They now were being offered with a snide literariness. Thus Sayers:

This gentleman, rather curly in the nose and fleshy about the eyelids . . .

And Sydney Horler:

The choicest collection of Hebraic types I have yet seen (even in New York) . . .

We were also hearing about a Russian club, where, according to Lord Peter Wimsey, 'cooking's beastly, the men don't shave . . .' Also 'a brotherhood of Indian frauds' joyfully reported by a Ronald Knox character to have been taken away by the police 'in a suitably coloured Maria', and characters described by Leslie Charteris's Simon Templar as 'the birds with the fat cigars and the names in -heim and -stein, who juggle the finances of this cockeyed world'.

One wonders why the poor old Chinese were so confidently expected by the crime writers of the inter-war years to inspire fear and dislike in their readers. They clearly were playing upon a deeply implanted association in the public mind between Asia and things unclean and creepy.

One reason for this attitude could have been the spate of political and pseudo-religious propaganda that sought to justify British intervention in the Far East for imperialist and commercial purposes. This was sustained during much of Victoria's reign and afterwards, and no conquest ever inspired a campaign of more bitter vilification than that directed against the unfortunate inhabitants of China by school historians, missionary societies, and Sunday school superintendents. Readers grew up already conditioned to accept and enjoy the Fu Manchu type of xenophobia that permeated crime fiction.

They were prepared also to ascribe to Oriental sources that much publicized traffic in drugs which followed the 1914/18 war. The very mention of heroin or cocaine, the two most favoured narcotics at that time, was enough to send a shiver of excitement up the public spine. Newspapers kept the shivers going. They were helped by the fact that drug-taking, being expensive, was mainly the indulgence of wealthy and often well-connected people. Every now and again some top-drawer addict would 'tell all' for one Sunday newspaper or another. Behind the portentous language of these hack-ghosted confessions was precious little information. However, in the compost of imprecision there grew an almost superstitious dread which an innocent and ignorant readership found very enjoyable.

Predictably, drug-trafficking became one of the main subjects of the detective story, taking its place alongside blackmail, will-jumping, larceny of emeralds and concealment of fraud.

Edgar Wallace

Characters usually referred to narcotics as 'the stuff'. The use of this casually knowledgeable expression was one of the many devices employed by authors ill qualified to venture into exact definition. So was the frequent mention of 'pin-point pupils' – seemingly the sole symptom of drug-taking familiar to the public of the 1930s.

In surprising contrast to the average detective story writer's vagueness concerning drugs, was his confident expertise in such esoteric fields as that of ancient weapons. Even the Humdrums – Julian Symons's felicitous name for the legion of middle-rank mystery writers who lacked the ingenuity and literary skill to compare with Nicholas Blake, Sayers, Christie, Francis Iles or Margery Allingham where plots or characterisation were concerned – could be relied upon to prove omniscient whenever a Florentine dagger or a Portuguese arquebus happened to be left around.

The device of making a plot turn upon some scrap of rare knowledge or highly technical information was growing very tiresome by the end of the period. So was the habit of some of the academic writers who had entered the lists – often to earn distinction – of larding their dialogue with over-clever common room chat. Even this, though, has its special interest now as an indication of the opinions and attitudes of an important section of the middle class forty years ago. Bitchiness, certainly, can be seen to be no latter-day import into our cloisters of learning. And does Lord Snow, it might be wondered, now find the sentiments in *Death Under Sail,* that early foray of his into crime fiction, as surprising as he must find its style?

The division between town and country, as it is drawn in the whodunnit literature of the inter-war years, is broad and deep. There appear to be no gradations of territory, no hinterland, no suburbs, even. As a general rule, the reader finds himself unmistakably in either a village or London's West End, the area described by Edgar Wallace as that 'where Somebodies live'.

The special image of the capital was calculated to give readers a pleasant sense of venturing among the wealthy, the daring, the witty and the wicked. It was an image that remained substantially unchanged throughout two decades, although some of its elements, such as the Bright Young Things and the Jazz Age with its flappers, flat chests and 'dickie' riding, were already fairly stale by the middle 1930s.

Especially faithful to the concept of a London where the only life worth noticing was nocturnal, confined to Belgravia, and led by men and women of impeccable dress sense and permanently fatuous conversation, were thriller writers exemplified

by Peter Cheyney. They were not numerous, but they were as diligent as they were undistinguished and they paved the way for the larger and more heavily promoted group of paperback authors who would eventually form the nearest approximation in this country to the Mickey Spillane industry. Forty years ago, they had to be content with what sexual frissons could be conveyed by a brutally held wrist or a hurled drink.

The approval of such goings on that was implicit in the writings of Mr Cheyney was not shared by the majority of crime novelists. The Humdrums, while dutifully contributing to the illusion of an exciting London night life, made it clear that their allegiance was to the moral code of the bank and the boarding school. References to the frequenters of night clubs included such adjectives as 'sleek', 'bored', and even 'evil-looking'. The women in those questionable establishments were 'daringly dressed', according to Bruce Graeme, and watched cabaret turns 'more indecent then entertaining'.

A very different tone was adopted towards the members of the same social class who eschewed the illicit delights of Chemin de Fer and after-hours drinking in favour of Bridge and Martinis in Eaton Square or Hyde Park Mansions.

Thus does detective story writer Ralph Trevor, present to us a society hostess:

'She is rather wonderful,' Sinclair owned. 'I have heard her described as one of the most efficient women in the whole of London. She possesses a perfect genius for marshalling the requisite ingredients for a successful house party.'

And here is Lord Peter Wimsey, epitome of all that Dorothy L. Sayers considered admirable in the upper crust male:

'His primrose-coloured hair was so exquisite a work of art that to eclipse it with his glossy hat was like shutting up the sun in a shrine of polished jet . . .'

Margery Allingham's detecting hero had a pedigree so impressive that his mother's name, though whispered off-stage, so to speak, was never divulged to the readers. His club also had to remain anonymous, although we are granted the information that it was one of the most exclusive in the world.

The implication discernible in the work of almost all the crime writers of the inter-war period was that only people with money were worth writing about. Even Edgar Wallace, who could never be accused of lacking the common touch, apparently accepted as perfectly normal the independent means and exclusive address of Mr J. G. Reeder, his 'Detective to the Public Prosecutor's Office', to say nothing of the private income of six thousand pounds a year enjoyed by a mere policeman, Socrates Smith.

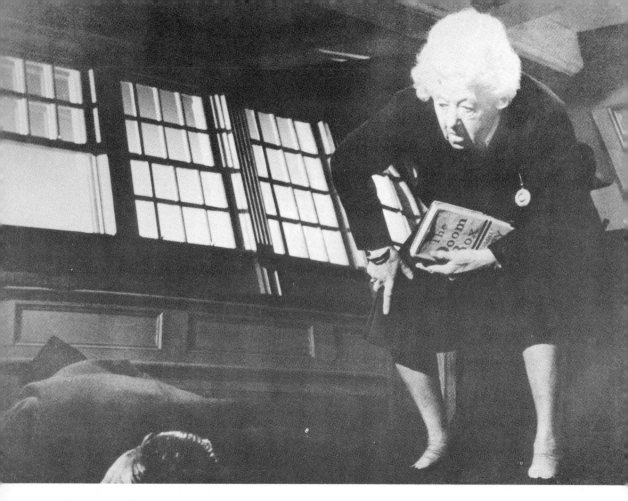

Margaret Rutherford as
Agatha Christie's Miss Marple
in the film *Murder Ahoy*

It is to the credit of Agatha Christie that she managed to maintain her steady and considerable output of mystery novels without having to invoke the exoticism of wealth. She was far too preoccupied with the convolutions of her plots to indulge in the sort of hero worship that put Miss Sayers in constant danger of literary hernia.

Private incomes do abound in Mrs Christie's books, but they are far more likely to be small pensions – such as that which supported Hercule Poirot, late of the Belgian police – than manorial rents. Her characters are in the main professional people, retired officers, spinster companions, clergymen, teachers, with a few oddities such as artists, thrown in as material for light relief or red herringry. There are precious few scions of the nobility; but no one, either, who could be categorised as working class, with the exception of what had come to be standard fictional furniture by the 1930s, those domestic servants, postmen, garage hands, milkmen and so on, whose functions were simply to bear witness and provide amusement.

The Christie, or 'cosy' school of detective fiction was, in fact, as distinctly middle class a phenomenon as the garden suburb or the home-made cake shop. A typical setting would be a community located in the kind of village of which commuters dream, self-contained and substantially self-sufficient, but picturesque and just remote enough from town (London, naturally) to give the illusion of rural security.

Such a village would have a Women's Institute, a hall, a well-attended church, an inn with reasonable accommodation for the occasional visitor from the Yard, a library perhaps (almost every author of the period makes mention of this praiseworthy amenity, and who is to blame him?) and some shops. There would be reasonable bus and train services for the making of suspicious journeys or the provision of time-table alibis.

There would dwell in the neighbourhood a number of well-off people, distinguished by their invariable habit of dressing for dinner. The middle layer of the population would be a mixture of the genteel, the comfy, and the making-both-ends-meet. Working folk would constitute the remainder, static in ways and in thought; either cheerfully deferential or resentful and mischievous; but all expressing themselves in a curious wot-I-always-sez-is kind of argot.

Characters would not be distinguishable as individual human beings, but class would be easily enough identifiable. A brigadier would speak as a brigadier was traditionally expected to speak; a vicar would use vicar talk; a wealthy invalid would whine away in the appropriate terms that a hundred or a thousand books already had made familiar.

Dulcie Gray, herself a crime writer, as Miss Marple in the stage version of *A Murder is Announced*

There would exist for these people no really intractable problems, nothing sordid, nothing mentally challenging. One or two would get murdered; the rest would pass under suspicion in a formal sarabande of investigation until the unmasking of the murderer and his or her disposal at the hands of the law. This last would be implied merely; executions were no more considered a fit subject for direct treatment than were autopsies; indeed, it is interesting to note how often the tidy alternative of suicide was invoked.

The 'cosy' brand of crime fiction has been criticised as two-dimensional. But it is doubtful if it could have offered what it did – relaxation, diversion and reassurance – if it had possessed that third dimension which imparts to the reader something of the effect of real experience.

Here was a gentle landscape of acceptance and what people who do not care much for explorative thought call 'common sense', featuring neither dramatic heights nor abysses of

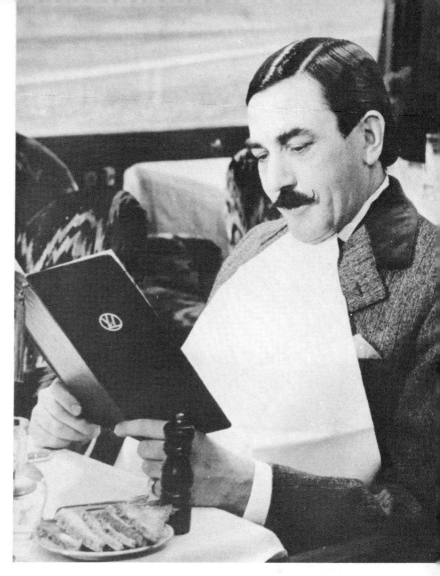

Three portrayals of Hercule Poirot. (*Opposite*) Peter Ustinov in the 1978 film *Death On the Nile*; (*above*) Charles Laughton in the 1928 stage version of *The Murder of Roger Ackroyd* called *Alibi*; (*right*) Albert Finney in the 1974 film *Murder on the Orient Express*

desperation. It was, in a sense, a playground, a sort of maze, at the centre of whose neat little hedges awaited a figure labelled The Murderer. One was not scared of meeting this unknown. There was in the pursuit of the puzzle's winding paths a cheerful curiosity, very different from the feeling of dread inspired by the anonymous slayer in the real world.

The ritual of investigation, deduction and inevitable solution, had several effects. It confirmed as desirable the rule of law and decency. The rendering harmless of the criminal at the end of each book seemed somehow to cancel out the deaths and distress that had gone before. It all made the world seem right, tight, and as we were. And that, in a Golden Age of which the glister was lamentably ephemeral, was a devoutly desired delusion.

3

Dorothy L. Sayers:
From puzzle to novel

by P. D. James

It is a safe assumption that any aficionado of the classical detective story, asked to name the six best writers in the genre, would include the name of Dorothy L. Sayers, yet, paradoxically, there is no other writer of the golden era who provokes such a strong and often opposing response from readers and critics alike. To her admirers she is the writer who did more than any other to make the detective story intellectually respectable and to change it from an ingenious but lifeless sub-literary puzzle into a specialised branch of fiction with serious claims to be judged as a novel. To her detractors she is outrageously snobbish, intellectually arrogant (certainly no other detective writer has produced an important clue in the form of a letter written entirely in French which she does not deign to translate for the benefit of her readers), pretentious and occasionally so dull as to be unreadable. But there can be no doubt of her influence both on succeeding writers and on the genre itself and it is probably best expressed in an introduction she wrote to an anthology of short stories *Tales of Detection* published in 1936:

No kind of fiction can survive for very long cut off from the great interests of humanity and from the mainstream of contemporary literature. We can now handle the mechanical elements of the plot with ease of long practice; we have yet to discover the best way of combining these with the serious artistic treatment of the psychological elements, so that the intellectual and the common man can find common ground for enjoyment in the mystery novel as they once did in Greek or Elizabethan tragedy.

It is possible that Dorothy L. Sayers chose the detective story because its constraints and preoccupations fulfilled some need in her own personality, a reconciliation of her passionate romanticism with the dominant intellect, but also because she recognised both its commercial attractions and its potentialities. Certainly she brought to her chosen task an impressive and trained intelligence, ingenuity, style, energy, enthusiasm and wit. She is one of the few writers of the Golden Age of the 1930s who is still widely read and who appeals to a generation other than her own. Undoubtedly the television series of her novels has had its effect in introducing them to a wider public, and the present cult for nostalgia has probably helped. But her virtues are stalwart and will endure and her defects, notably the snobbery and class and racial consciousness which intrude distastefully, particularly in *Have his Carcase,* can be viewed as symptomatic of her age rather than of a personal peculiarity or prejudice. They are extremely offensive to our present fashion in susceptibilities, just as it is possible that current crime novels' preoccupation with sadism and moral anarchy may be equally offensive to our grandchildren's generation.

(Previous page)
Dorothy L. Sayers in 1928

Two portrayals of Lord Peter Wimsey and Bunter. (*Opposite*) Robert Montgomery attended by Sir Seymour Hicks in the 1940 film *Busman's Honeymoon;* (*above*) Ian Carmichael with Glyn Houston in the 1974 BBC television version of *The Nine Tailors*

Those who are irritated by Dorothy L. Sayers (she was insistent on that 'L' in her name) frequently focus their dislike on her aristocratic detective, Lord Peter Wimsey. The choice of the younger son of a Duke as her protagonist must have offered a number of obvious attractions to a mystery writer. As a wealthy dilettante he would be able to pursue the clues without the boring necessity of earning a living; his title would pander to reader snobbery and to the obsessional fascination of the less privileged with the life style of the aristocracy, or with what they fancied that life style to be. He would have sufficient influence through his rank and wealth to be able to poke his nose with impunity into the affairs of others where less aristocratic noses would be speedily bloodied; and he could pay his helots to do the more boring work. One of the most risible aspects of the books and one which places them firmly in their age is the exaggerated and tender respect with which the professional police force regard the amateur sleuth. Chief Constables receive Wimsey with deference; detectives welcome his co-operation; Inspector Parker, who conveniently marries Wimsey's sister, is often little more than his brother-in-law's stooge. Miss Sayers provided Wimsey with all the appropriate upper class accoutrements. Educated at Eton (of course) and at Balliol, he took a First Class Degree in History, is a fine natural cricketer, a connoisseur of wine, food, and occasionally women, a virtuoso performer on the piano who can pass happily from Bach to a Scarlatti sonata without benefit of a score, and a discerning bibliophile. He is, of course, a phantasy figure. But is he any more a phantasy than the lean, cynical, wisecracking private eye on his long forages down the mean streets, or the psychologically maimed hero/victim of the modern espionage thriller?

Wimsey's manservant, Bunter, was obviously derived from Jeeves and has all Jeeves's efficiency and omniscience but without his innate consciousness of superiority to his master. Even when ordered away in search of clues in *Have his Carcase* Bunter is preoccupied with Lord Peter's comfort:

'Your Lordship will forgive me for reminding you that it is advisable to remove the links from the shirt cuff before despatching the garment to the laundry. It gives me great anxiety to feel that I shall not be at hand to attend to the matter myself on Monday.'

The hurrying throng of 1930 wage earners, who perforce removed their own cuff links, streaming into Baker Street station to catch the 6.30 back to mortgaged Metroland, harassed by the fear of unemployment, worried by the depression and gathering storms over Europe, must have escaped with relief into Lord Peter's opulent drawing room at 110A Piccadilly with its walls lined with first editions, its bowl of chrysanthemums on the grand piano and Bunter deferentially proffering the Cockburn '96. Wimsey's Piccadilly flat is as cosy and reassuring a refuge from the alarming world outside as is the claustrophobic sanctum at 221B Baker Street.

Perhaps because clue making so often involves the routine and minutiae of ordinary life no other form of popular writing tells us as much about the age in which it was written than does the detective story. For this reason the genre may survive when more pretentious literary forms are forgotten. For millions of readers Victorian London is Conan Doyle's fog shrouded Baker Street, and in Dorothy L. Sayers the sound and feel, the mood and speech of the 30s seems to rise from the page. Her books are strewn with the sad human detritus of the 1914–18 war; the gallant or pathetic spinsters like Miss Climpson and Miss Twitterton, the war wounded and disillusioned heroes of the Bellona Club, the lonely women in cheap hotels seeking solace and excitement in spiritualism in *Strong Poison*. To read *Murder must Advertise* is to know precisely what it was to work in a commercial office in the City when £4 a week was a wage on which a copy-writer could live in comfort in central London and even make some show of tagging along with the bright young things. The central plot of *The Unpleasantness at the Bellona Club* hinges on the certainty that the whole country would be still and silent for precisely two minutes at the eleventh hour of the eleventh day of the eleventh month. General Fentiman in the same book could spend a day at his club paying for his luncheon and the taxi home with a ten shilling note. Harriet Vane could stay in theatrical lodgings in *Have His Carcase* for twelve shillings a week all found, and Wimsey in *Busman's Honeymoon* paid 204 shillings (£10.20 in modern money) for a dozen bottles of vintage Port. As Miss Twitterton gasped:

'Seventeen shillings a bottle! Oh, it's impossible! It's . . . it's wicked!'

But some of the sartorial detail seems *outré* even for the 1930s. Would Lord Peter in *Busman's Honeymoon* really have attended a village funeral in top hat and morning suit, even if the corpse had been discovered with its head bashed in at the foot of his cellar steps? And Harriet Vane's eminently unsuitable outfit for picnicking in *Have His Carcase* of a skirt which waved tempestuously about her ankles, an oversized hat of which one side obscured her face and tickled her shoulder while the other was turned back to reveal a bunch of black ringlets, high heeled beige shoes and sheer silk stocking with embroidered gloves, the whole reminiscent of a cigarette card of a simpering 1930 movie queen, is hardly excusable by the fact that Harriet was setting out to vamp a suspected murderer.

Although Dorothy L. Sayers was as adept as any of her contemporaries in the tricks of her trade, the manipulation of train timetables, the drawing of red herrings skilfully across trails, the devising of alibis which depended on clocks, tides, secret codes and mysterious foreigners, all her novels have a central idea which is both ingenious and original even if occasionally, it strains belief. In *The Unpleasantness at the Bellona Club* and *Have His Carcase* the plot depends on the accurate determination of the time of death. *The Nine Tailors, Strong Poison* and *Unnatural Death* contain original methods of murder, although two of them are highly unlikely to be effective in practice.

Although she wrote with vigour, humour and panache, hers was not a strongly creative talent. She set her books in places with which she was familiar, Galloway in *The Five Red Herrings,* the Fen country in *The Nine Tailors,* Oxford in

Gaudy Night and in the London of Bloomsbury bed-sitting rooms, fringe clubs and offices in which she herself had lived and worked. Most of her more successful and convincing characters, notably the staff of Pym's Publicity in *Murder Must Advertise* and the Rev. Venables in *The Nine Tailors* seem to have been drawn from real life. Those who are not, especially servants, police officers and the working class, are often little more than stereotypes.

She was not a didactic writer – it is arguable whether any novelist should be – and *Gaudy Night*, the only book in which she deliberately set out 'to say things which, in a confused way, I had been wanting to say all my life' about the overwhelming importance of the integrity of the mind is not among her most successful detective novels, although it has an attraction for lovers of Oxford and for those romantics primarily interested in the progress of the love affair between Peter Wimsey and Harriet Vane.

The difficulty with a detective hero who is, himself, something of a stereotype is that his writer eventually outgrows him and comes to regret the earlier crudities of her creation and the restrictions which these can impose on the psychological development of the character. Dorothy L. Sayers is not the only detective writer whose hero changes almost out of recognition as book succeeds book. It is difficult to reconcile the Peter Wimsey of *Gaudy Night,* 'wearing cap and gown like any orthodox Master of Arts, presenting every appearance of having piously attended the University Sermon, and now talking mild academic shop with two Fellows of All Souls and the Master of Balliol' with a monocled, silly ass, man-about-town who occasionally bursts out into a caricature of Bertie Wooster in the earlier books. But by the time she wrote *Gaudy Night,* Miss Sayers, like her alter ego, had become dangerously enamoured of her aristocratic sleuth. This is said to be an occupational hazard for the female writer, but no more of a risk, one would have thought, than the male writer runs if tempted to emulate the exploits, sexual or acrobatic, of his more audacious heroes.

Dorothy L. Sayers helped to transform the detective story into the crime novel, but she was an innovator of style and intention not of form. She worked within the well-worn convention of a central mystery, a circle of suspects, an egregiously talented detective and a solution which the reader could arrive at by a process of logical deduction from clues which were presented to him with deceptive cunning but with essential fairness. The two most notable writers in this genre to succeed her were both women and both worked within this

Dame Ngaio Marsh

central convention. Margery Allingham (1904–1966) also portrayed aspects of the age in which she wrote but with a more ironic detachment and more consciously than did Dorothy L. Sayers. *Flowers for the Judge* deals with publishing; *Dancers in Mourning* with the frenetic world of the theatrical star; *The Fashion in Shrouds* with the ephemeral mystique of a high fashion house. She had considerable descriptive gifts especially for places, the seedier squares of North West London, decaying post-war streets, the salt marshes of the Essex coast. Like Dorothy L. Sayers she created in Albert Campion a snobbish detective, 'An amateur who never used his real name and title', and one who developed psychological subtlety and, indeed, even changed his appearance as she widened the scope of her creative talent. Many critics would rate *The Tiger in the Smoke* (1952), the story of a manhunt in fog shrouded London, one of the best half dozen detective stories ever written. The characters of Jack Havoc the murderer and the gentle but implacable Canon Avril refute criticism that the great absolutes of good and evil are outside the range of the detective novelist.

Ngaio Marsh (1899–   ) has justified her own statement that 'The mechanics of a detective story may be shamelessly contrived but the writing need not be'. It has been said that the formula for a successful detective story is 50 per cent good detection, 25 per cent character, and 25 per cent what the writer knows best. Ngaio Marsh, a New Zealander, makes good use of her own distinguished career in her country's theatre by setting some of her most successful books, notably *Enter a Murderer, Opening Night* and *Death at the Dolphin* in the world of the drama, making excellent use of backstage intrigue and giving a lively account of the problems and mechanics of running a professional company of players. She is less concerned with the psychology of her characters than is Margery Allingham and the lengthy interrogations by her urbane detective Superintendent Alleyn have their *longueurs*. But both women are novelists not merely fabricators of ingenious puzzles. Both seek, not always successfully, to reconcile the conventions of the classical detective story with the novel of social realism.

Any female writer of mysteries gets used to the question, particularly from American readers, 'Why is it that respectable English women are so good at murder?' This somewhat invidious enquiry is, perhaps not surprising in view of the pre-eminence of Agatha Christie, Dorothy L. Sayers, Margery Allingham and Ngaio Marsh, all of them experts in the gentle art of violent death. And, with women, it usually is the gentle art. They agree with W. H. Auden that the single body on the drawing room floor is far more shocking than a dozen bullet-ridden corpses on one of Raymond Chandler's mean city streets. Not for them the sardonic, wisecracking private eye who can never burst through a door without finding either a corpse, a blonde, or a gun and sometimes all three on the other side of it. Women mystery writers are chiefly concerned with malice domestic, the stresses, tensions, irritations and hatreds which can fester in a close community and can erupt into the ultimate crime. Perhaps it is because women are more interested in violent emotions than in violent actions that they deal in poison rather than guns, with kitchen knives rather than high explosives. 'Stands the church clock at ten to three/And is there arsenic still for tea?'

The criticism of Dorothy L. Sayers and of her contemporaries is a criticism of the mainstream detective story which she deepened and widened and yet which continued after her fundamentally unaltered. The case against the genre as typified by her is formidable. Firstly, that the detective story trivialises the conflict between good and evil reducing it to a cosy pseudo-battle between the forces of law and lawlessness, conformity and rebellion. That it is fundamentally without compassion dealing perfunctorily with tragedy and the problem of suffering. That all psychological interest in character is subjugated to serve the interest of the plot. That it is the produce of a snobbish and a basically puritanical society defending the inalienable right of the possessor to defend his possessions against the greed and envy of predators and one in which the working class, including some policemen, are treated as buffoons or simpletons, mere foils to the brilliance of the omniscient detective. Much of this criticism is as perverse and inappropriate as criticising P. G. Wodehouse because Bertie Wooster has an imperfect appreciation of the Marxist dialectic or the Drones Club does not accurately reflect the class struggle inherent in a capitalist economy. But, more seriously, a genre which rests on the fundamental belief that wilful killing is wrong and that every human being, no matter how unpleasant, inconvenient or worthless his life may be, has a right to live it to the last natural moment, needs no particular apology in an age in which gratuitous violence and arbitrary death have become common.

A glance at any short list for the Crime Writers' Association's annual awards shows the extraordinary wide range today of crime writing and the distance which the detective story, now only one small part of the genre, has travelled since the days when every plot contained a butler and full supporting cast of domestic suspects, when the reader was presented with a map of the Grange with the bedrooms neatly marked, when alibis depended on reliable train time-tables and the final denouement invariably took place in the library after dinner usually with everyone in full evening dress. In those so called golden years ingenuity of plot was everything; style, atmosphere, subtlety of characterisation and social awareness, all were subordinate to the puzzle. Today most detective writers aim to achieve a mystery which is also a good novel, where the victim is more than a blood-stained cadaver, the suspects are people not stereotypes, where the setting is described with economy but realism, and where the central puzzle still intrigues but doesn't dominate. The nineteen-thirties detective story with its deference to hierarchy, its comfortable orthodoxies, has given place to the psychological subtleties and moral ambiguities of the crime novel. Here, in the words of Robert Browning, we are indeed 'on the dangerous edge of things'. Here murder may be motiveless, hunter and hunted, hero and victim are one, corruption sits in the citadel of law, and there is no longer a neat and logical solution in the last chapter – not even for a Lord Peter Wimsey.

Further Reading

Little has been written about Sayers, Allingham and Marsh outside such general studies as Howard Haycraft's *Murder for Pleasure* (Peter Davies; 1942) and Julian Symons' *Bloody Murder: from the detective story to the crime novel: a history* (Faber, 1972; Penguin Books, 1974).

Such A Strange Lady: a biography of Dorothy L. Sayers by Janet Hitchman (New English Library, 1976) is the only such biography to date.

Tales of Detection (Everyman Library, J. M. Dent 1936, reprinted 1961, o.p.) has a long introduction by Dorothy L. Sayers which admirably sets out her view of the development of the detective story. It has been reprinted in *The Art of the Mystery Story,* edited by Howard Haycraft (Simon Schuster, 1946).

Thrillers: genesis and structure of a popular genre by Jerry Palmer (Arnold, 1978).

From the Golden Age to Mean Streets

The writers of the 'Golden Age' of the Twenties and Thirties set out to entertain, and they often succeeded admirably. The books of the Twenties were essentially games played between author and reader, at their best highly ingenious logical puzzles. The author attempts to mislead the reader by diverting suspicion from the guilty character while at the same time placing all the relevant clues and motives in the text. The reader will naturally feel cheated if the author withholds a vital piece of information only to reveal it triumphantly at the last minute. It was the importance of this game-playing element in the books that led Monsignor Ronald Knox to devise the original rules for the Detection Club.

The shortcomings of the 'Golden Age' are apparent with hindsight. Raymond Chandler's famous attack on the classic detective story in *The Simple Art of Murder* did not appear until 1944. In the Thirties the form was vigorous enough to attract much new talent. Some of the writers, like Nicholas Blake, the poet Cecil Day-Lewis, and Michael Innes, brought wit and freshness to the form, while others, like Margery Allingham and Ngaio Marsh, worked their own

---

The Initiation Ceremony of the Detection Club

The club was founded in 1932 and is still flourishing. Originally membership was confined to detective story writers. This is part of the initiation ritual new members had to undergo.

President: Is it your firm desire to become a member of the Detection Club?

Initiate: That is my desire.

President: Do you promise that your detectives shall well and truly detect the crimes presented to them, using those wits which it may please you to bestow upon them and not placing reliance on, nor making use of, Divine Revelation, Feminine Intuition, Mumbo Jumbo, Jiggery Pokery, Coincidence or the Act of God.

Initiate: I do.

President: Do you solemnly swear never to conceal a vital clue from the reader?

Initiate: I do.

President: Do you promise to observe a seemly moderation in the use of Gangs, Conspiracies, Death Rays, Ghosts, Hypnotism, Trap Doors, Chinamen, Super-Criminals and Lunatics – and utterly and for ever forswear Mysterious Poisons Unknown to Science?

Initiate: I do.

President: Will you honour the King's English?

Initiate: I will.

President: Do you, as you hope to increase your Sales, swear to observe faithfully all these promises which you have made, so long as you are a Member of the Club?

Initiate: All this I solemnly do swear. And I do furthermore promise and undertake to be loyal to the Club, neither purloining nor disclosing any plot or secret communicated to me before publication by any Member, whether under the influence of drink or otherwise.

President: If there be any Member present who objects to the Proposal, let him or her so declare.

(pause)

Do you then acclaim this detective story writer a Member of the Club?

All: Yes.

President: You are duly elected a Member of the Detection Club, and if you fail to keep your promise, may other writers anticipate your plots, may your publisher do you down in your contracts, may strangers sue you for libel, may your pages swarm with misprints and may your sales continually diminish. Amen.

Initiate: Amen.

Anthony Berkeley

Michael Innes

John Dickson Carr

Rex Stout

variations on the formula. With the newer writers a greater degree of reality was allowed to enter the books, and their detectives lost some of their infallibility. There were other signs that a change was coming: Both Dorothy L. Sayers and Anthony Berkeley had made perceptive comments about the need for the crime novel to progress, to become something more than simply a puzzle. Berkeley was a successful writer of traditional stories, but he fulfilled his own prophecy when he published, under the name of Francis Iles, two remarkable books, *Malice Aforethought* and *Before The Fact*. Both books are a radical departure from the conventions of the 'Golden Age', starting with the first paragraph of each. In both cases the murderer is named at the beginning of the story. There is no puzzle to solve, instead the books depend on the realism and psychological depth of the characters. These two books are quite different to anything he wrote as Anthony Berkeley, and although they were well received, they did not have any immediately noticeable effect on the course of the crime novel. The change was to come later from America.

The American writers of the 'Golden Age' were at first very similar to their British contemporaries. The books of John Dickson Carr, who spent a considerable period in Britain and was honorary secretary of the Detection Club, have a very English style and are frequently set in England. His detective hero, Dr Gideon Fell, has a strong physical resemblance to G. K. Chesterton. S. S. Van Dine created Philo Vance, a hero who surpasses the British creations in both snobbery and omniscience and who was actually Oxford educated. The books were enormously successful and for a while dominated the Ameri-

can best-seller lists. Rex Stout created the monstrously fat and almost immobile detective Nero Wolfe and his tough, active and sometimes aggressive assistant Archie Goodwin. There were many other American writers and their books have a distinct style, often sharper and more brittle than the British writers. It would be impossible in any survey, however brief, not to make a special mention of Ellery Queen. The Ellery Queen books are amongst the finest puzzles that the Golden Age produced. They are brilliant exercises in rational deduction with all the clues presented fairly and clearly to the reader. The partnership that produced Ellery Queen, Frederic Dannay and Manfred B. Lee, was outstandingly successful, and as well as the many books they also produced the *Ellery Queen Mystery Magazine,* which first appeared in 1941. This magazine has done much to keep the short story alive and to encourage new writers. The selection of stories for the magazine has never been confined to any one area of crime fiction, but has reflected the changes that have taken place over the years.

Manfred B. Lee and Frederic Dannay (Ellery Queen)

The American Golden Age

ELLERY QUEEN: *In the beginning when we belonged to the so-called Golden Age of detective stories, our main emphasis was on plot, on things like ingenuity, surprise, suspense. But we soon began to realise that the old Golden Age was probably coming to an end and that a new type of story would be needed, and this was of course also accelerated by the growing popularity of the 'Black Mask', or hard-boiled school. So towards the end of the Golden Age we began to change, and it was at that time that we wanted to do more serious work. So we decided to do it against the background of a typical American small town. This change was not only a change in approach but a change in style too, because what we were really trying to do was to take the framework of the pure detective story and adapt it to a more serious approach, like the serious novel or the novel of manners.*

From an interview in the *Crime Writers* television series.

When the major change did take place in the crime story it came, not from the established writers trying to break new ground and not from any of the established publishers. It was the American pulp magazines that gave birth to the new form, and to a new type of hero.

Catering for a totally different section of the public, these magazines attracted writers who shared with the readers a harsh view of life where violence and corruption ruled. To some extent these magazines dramatised what the newspapers reported, the increasing power of the gangsters and the corruption of police and politicians. It was in these magazines that the hard-boiled detective was born, a man no better than the next man, and who often put his trust in a gun, but a man who couldn't be bought. The fast action and harshness of the stories demanded a writing style that was closer to the way that people spoke on the streets and had no room for affectation or indulgence. Action, taut dialogue and excitement was the order of the day, and that was what the writers provided.

Carroll John Daly is credited with the creation of the first hardboiled detective with his character Race Williams, but the outstanding contribution to the development of this new field was made by the *Black Mask* magazine. This was a popular fiction magazine that had been founded by H. L. Mencken and George Jean Nathan to subsidize their more sophisticated *Smart Set*. Its literary background gave the magazine an edge over its competitors, and in 1922 Dashiell Hammett published his first story in its pages.

H. L. Mencken

A *Black Mask* dinner in Los Angeles in 1936. (*Bottom row*) Arthur Barnes, John K. Butler, Tod Hunter Ballard, Horace McCoy, Norbert Davis. (*Top row*) an unknown party-crasher, Raymond Chandler, Herbert Stinson, Dwight Babcock, Eric Taylor and Dashiell Hammett.

About Hammett

ROSS MACDONALD: *I started reading Hammett when I was about 14 years old, and I remember the first time I ever picked up a Hammett book and read a few pages, it was in a tobacco shop that had a lending library in down town Kitchener, Ontario. And although the book was about an American city, it told me more, in a sense, about the real life and particularly the under-life and the levels of life in a small city than anything else I'd ever read.*

GAVIN LYALL: *I think that, at the time Hammett was writing, which was during the Depression, during Prohibition, you couldn't be unaware of what was going on in America. If you had any sensitivity at all you would know that there were a lot of people starving, a lot of people out of work – that there were a lot of people being shot down by rich gangsters. But I don't think that Hammett thought there was a political solution available. He may have thought of a more moral, social solution. He just believed that 'the huddled masses yearning to be free' was what America was about.*

From interviews in the *Crime Writers* television series.

4
Dashiell Hammett:
The Onlie Begetter

by Julian Symons

THE LIFE

Dashiell Hammett's life and works have a legendary fame in the United States. A novel has been written about his early adult life in San Francisco, and Jason Robards recently played him on the screen in *Julia*. In Britain he is less known than his lineal follower Raymond Chandler, and in an account of him it seems worth briefly recounting his life, which was much more interesting than those of most crime writers, and also has a direct connection with his work.

Samuel Dashiell Hammett was born in Maryland in 1894. His parentage was mixed Scottish and French, and the emphasis in Dashiell should be on the second syllable (it is derived from De Chiel), a difficulty in pronunciation eliminated in Hammett's lifetime by abbreviation of the name to Dash. He left school at 14, and then experienced what sometimes seems a standard American practical education by doing rough jobs like those of freight clerk, stevedore and nail-machine operator, before finding work as a Pinkerton detective. He spent four years as a Pinkerton man before enlisting in the Army. There he contracted tuberculosis, and for the rest of his life had intermittent struggles with the disease.

In 1919 he went back to his Pinkerton job, and in the following year married a nurse at the hospital from which he had been discharged with his file marked: 'Maximum improvement reached'. He was involved as a detective in the Fatty Arbuckle case, which he later characterised as a

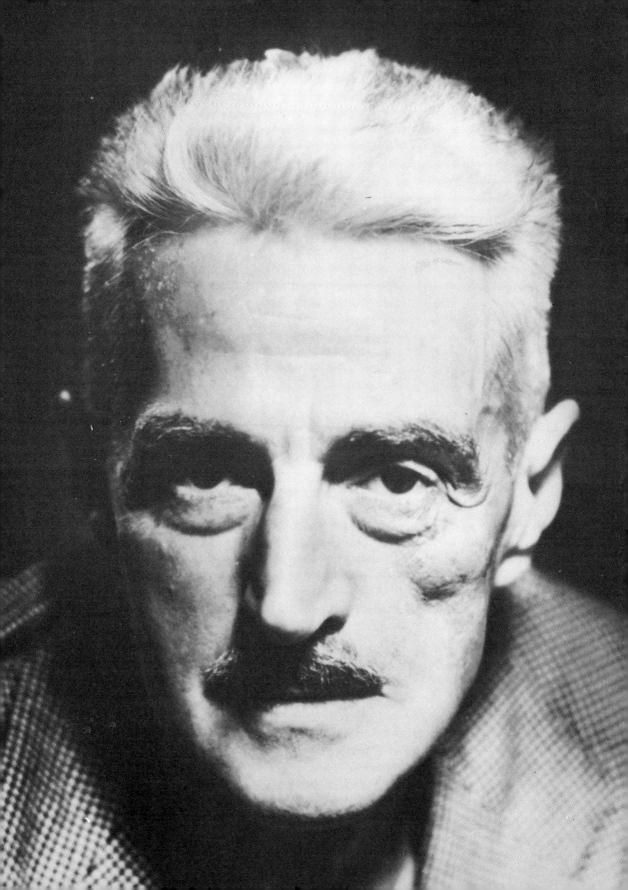

frame-up. In 1922 his first short stories were published, one of them in a newish pulp magazine named *Black Mask*. He used for these first stories a name which suggests the self-dramatising and secretive elements of his character: Peter Collinson. A Peter Collins was at one time American criminal slang for a nobody – so at least Hammett said, although the slang dictionaries I have consulted do not endorse him – so that Peter Collinson was nobody's son. By this time he had parted from his wife and small daughter, and was drinking hard. Later, when he had achieved a measure of success they rejoined him, and he had another daughter, but the marriage had ended long before his divorce in 1937.

Nobody's son was soon replaced by the name of Dashiell Hammett. It quickly became clear to the editor and readers of *Black Mask* that Hammett's stories about a small fat detective called simply the Continental Op, the Continental being the name of his agency, were superior to other work in the magazine in their knowledge and their style. The Op was based on a man named Wright in Pinkerton's Baltimore office, and the approach to realism in the Op's assignments and his attitude was something new. So were the direct suggestions of graft in American life in some of the stories.

For seven years Hammett made no more than a reasonable living from writing short crime stories about the Continental Op, mostly for *Black Mask*. Two novels, *Red Harvest* and *The Dain Curse,* appeared first in the magazine and then in revised form as novels, without outstanding success. Then in 1930, with the publication of *The Maltese Falcon,* Hammett became famous. The book went through more than twenty hard-cover printings in a few years. It was filmed in 1931 and again by John Huston ten years later, with Humphrey Bogart, Mary Astor and Sydney Greenstreet playing the parts originally acted – and acted more faithfully than critics have granted – by Richardo Cortez, Bebe Daniels and Dudley Digges.

Hammett described himself in a letter of this time as 'long and lean and grey-headed and very lazy . . . no ambition, no recreations'. He might have listed drinking and gambling as recreations, but perhaps he considered them as his lifetime occupation. Now, as the money poured in, he felt no need to go on working. He wrote two more books, *The Glass Key* (1931) and *The Thin Man* (1934) plus a small handful of short stories. Apart from that he went to Hollywood and saw his books made into films, with the Thin Man providing a whole series, a couple of them from his original screenplays. The money came in, he went on drinking, he met the youthful Lillian Hellman who recalled that at their first meeting he was recovering from

(Opposite) two film treatments
of *The Maltese Falcon*.
(Above) Humphrey Bogart as
Sam Spade, Peter Lorre as Joel
Cairo, Mary Astor as Brigid
O'Shaughnessy and Sydney
Greenstreet as Gutman in
John Huston's classic version
of 1941; (below) the much
altered *Satan Met a Lady* of
1936 with Arthur Treacher,
Warren William as the
detective called Ted Shane,
Bette Davis as the girl, and
Alison Skipworth playing Mme.
Barrabas, a transformation
of the Gutman character

a five-day drunk. They lived together, and he encouraged her to write. In 1934 her first stage play, *The Children's Hour,* was a triumphant success. The beginning of her career marked the end of Hammett's. He lived for another twenty-seven years, but never completed any other work. His life as a novelist had lasted for only six years, his whole life as a writer for twelve.

Why were there no more books or stories? The screen writer Nunnally Johnson, who knew Hammett well from the late Twenties, wrote to me that only somebody who 'had no expectation of being alive much beyond Thursday' could have spent himself and his money with such recklessness. Hammett told Johnson that he saw no reason to write when he not only had all the money he needed, but was assured of things staying that way until his life ended. In this he was mistaken, but the error was excusable. In the late Thirties it seemed likely that Sam Spade and Nick Charles would remain an endless source of revenue through radio and film series and cartoons, without Hammett having to provide more than an occasional idea and a few pieces of dialogue.

During these years Hammett had become involved in Hollywood Left-wing politics. It is an indication of the seriousness with which he took any moral stance that in September, 1942, he joined the U.S. Army Signal Corps. He was 48, and must have been far from fit, but he was accepted, and quickly volunteered for overseas duty. He was sent to the Aleutian Islands, and enjoyed life in this Siberian climate where, as he said, you had snow in the winter and mud in the summer, both up to your waist. He became known as Pop, ran a four-page daily paper for the troops, lent the boys money and paid their bar bills. He left the Army soon after the war ended, having contracted emphysema. There was little diminution in his income. The Hammett boom continued, with the reissue of the Continental Op stories in paperback. He took up drinking again in a big way, until he was rushed to hospital and warned that if he continued to drink he would be dead in a few months. He then gave up drinking completely.

He had twelve more years to live, and they cannot have been happy ones. He wrote one of the speeches in a play by Lillian Hellman, a speech in which a retired General talks of the turning point in a life, when you wipe out your past mistakes, 'do the work you've never done, think the way you'd never thought'. He deceived himself into believing that for him this time was now. He told his agent that a new book was on the way, and it was announced under the title of *December 1st,* and then as *There Was a Young Man.* But those books were never finished, perhaps were not even begun. The only work from

Lillian Hellman

this time ever printed, and that after his death, was an 18,000 word fragment of a novel called 'Tulip'. This Hemingwayesque piece is interesting chiefly because it shows Hammett's wish to move away from the kind of book that had made him famous. With 'Tulip' given up, he made no further attempt to write.

Before the writing of 'Tulip' he had gone to prison. He was a trustee for what was probably a Communist front organisation called the Civil Rights Congress. He was sent to prison for six months because he refused to tell a Congressional Committee the names of the contributors to the bail bond fund of the Congress. Lillian Hellman says that he had never been to the Congress office and did not know the name of a single contributor, but that he told her: 'If it were my life, I would give it for what I think democracy is and I don't let cops or judges tell me what I think democracy is.' Before discounting this as rhetoric, one should remember that, as Hammett's insistence on taking an active part in World War II showed, he was a man who in all important matters meant what he said. He wrote to Lillian Hellman that his prison job was cleaning bathrooms and that he cleaned them better than she had ever done. After coming out of prison he maddened her by saying that prison had not been so bad after all. But, as she reflected, she should have guessed that he 'would talk about his own time in jail the way many of us talk about college'.

Now the rich days were over. Although he was not one of the Hollywood Ten, and it is likely that his active connection with Communism was slight, Hammett was expelled from Hollywood favour. There were no more commissions to work on screenplays, his radio shows came off the air, the short-story collections went out of print and remained so. Joe McCarthy moved to have Hammett's books removed from the shelves of overseas libraries. He was sued for $140,000 in back taxes. He lived in a small ugly country cottage in Katonah, New York, moving out in the summer to Martha's Vineyard. He read a great deal, referred dismissively at times to his own books, became increasingly a recluse. In January 1961 he died, not from tuberculosis nor from alcoholism, but from an inoperable lung cancer discovered only two months before his death.

THE STYLE

It is difficult today to imagine the effect of reading Hammett short stories in the early or mid-nineteen twenties. Their plots were like others of the time, cramming as much violence as possible into a few pages, but the harsh tautness of the writing was new, and so was the hatred of corruption implicit in several stories. It was implicit, because Hammett never explained things. In these stories, as later in his books, he described events as they happened, without any comment by the author. Yet in spite of this deliberate detachment, an attitude is being conveyed in the opening sentence of the very early (1923) story 'House Dick':

The Montgomery Hotel's regular detective had taken his last week's rake-off from the hotel bootlegger in merchandise instead of cash, had drunk it down, had fallen asleep in the lobby, and had been fired.

The suggestion, without a word being positively said to that effect, is that if you are a detective you should be honest, you shouldn't get drunk, and if you are dishonest and drunk on the job, it is right that you should be fired. This code of honesty is extended to include all sorts of loyalties, loyalties which are always personal and not corporate. 'When a man's partner is killed he's supposed to do something about it,' Sam Spade says, and this is so even though the partner is fairly worthless. A similar code of loyalty between men is invoked in *The Glass Key,* although there all sorts of subtleties and contradictions are involved. There is also an ethic of the job. The princess in 'The Gutting of Couffignal' (1925) is certain that the Op won't shoot her if she tries to escape, and is astounded when he puts a bullet through her calf. This deliberate shooting of a woman must have outraged many readers at the time, and so must the Op's subsequent comment: 'You ought to have known I'd do it! Didn't I steal a crutch from a cripple?' Several of the early stories anticipate scenes in the novels, and the Op's treatment of the princess prefigures Spade's sending up of Brigid O'Shaughnessy.

The obvious likeness of style in early Hammett stories to those of Hemingway's first work has prompted arguments about possible influences. Hemingway could not have influenced Hammett because before 1925 he had published nothing in America, and it is not likely that early Hammett influenced Hemingway. Times of social change are often accompanied by changes in literary style, and the United States after World War I was a society in turmoil. The new world created by Prohibition, gangsterism and the loosening of sexual and social restrictions could not be adequately expressed in the prose of Edith Wharton, or even by the flat realism of Sinclair Lewis. Hammett and Hemingway used a prose which seemed to them at the time the only possible means of showing the world they were writing about: in Hemingway's case a world often of warfare and almost always of action, in Hammett's a violent, brutal and corrupt section of society. It was their intention to eliminate as far as possible the author's voice, in the hope that what emerged would be genuine and not synthetic. Hammett put it clearly a little later, in one of his rare literary pronouncements: 'The contemporary novelist's job is to take pieces of life and arrange them on paper. And the more direct their passage from street to paper the more lifelike they should turn out . . . The novelist must know how things happen – not how they are remembered in later years – and he must write them down that way.'

One must not claim too much for the short stories. Hammett himself thought little of them, and allowed them to be reprinted only after constant pressure by publishers. Their merits are those of sharpness, hardness, bareness, but the determination to cut out unnecessary adjectives and to avoid purple passages means that the author is sometimes not much more than a photographic recorder. The style is interesting, particularly in comparison with what was being published elsewhere, but it is deliberately drained of colour, so that even scenes of action tend to be played down rather than up.

Such personal stylistic notes as Hammett permits himself in the stories come usually in the openings. 'It was a wandering daughter job . . . I was the only one who left the train at Farewell . . . Sam Spade said "My name is Ronald Ames".' The turning point that Hammett wrote about much later in fact came for him in the middle Twenties, when he became discontented with what he was doing, and realised that it would be possible for him to write a full-length book in which he could criticise the society in which he lived through the medium of a violent story about crime.

The book was *Red Harvest,* which was printed in four long sections in *Black Mask* at the end of 1927 and the beginning of 1928, and was published as a book in the following year. It was revised page by page for book publication, always with a view to making it more colloquial. The result is a novel remarkable in its attitude towards violence and towards the police, and in the way it conveys through the acid prose the stench of society in Personville, which is called Poisonville. This is a town in which all of the police are crooked, not just one or two. When Noonan the police chief has one of the gangsters holed up so that he can't escape, the gangster gives money to a subordinate and tells him to buy his way out. After he has done so a uniformed cop holds the back gate open for the gangsters, muttering nervously 'Hurry it up boys, please', and a car takes them to safety. The Op, who is with the gangsters, is characteristically casual in telling us the car's origin: 'The last I saw of it was its police department licence plate vanishing around a corner.' The Op cleans up Poisonville by playing one gangster against another, so that they are wiped out. The end of the story offers little cheer to believers in good government. Personville, with all the gangsters dead (there are 28 violent deaths in the book by my count, but it is not easy to be exact) is 'developing into a sweet-smelling and thornless bed of roses', but it is under martial law. Bill Quint, the red-tied union organiser introduced in the opening chapter, has given the place up as a bad job.

In *Red Harvest* Hammett also for the first time gave full play to his strong visual sense and his skill in conveying character through visual description. Here is old Elihu Willsson, 'the czar of Poisonville':

The old man's head was small and almost perfectly round under its close-cut crop of white hair. His ears were too small and plastered too flat to the sides of his head to spoil the spherical effect. His nose also was small, carrying down the curve of his bony forehead. Mouth and chin were straight lines chopping the sphere off. Below them a short thick neck ran down into white pyjamas between square meaty shoulders. One of his arms was outside the covers, a short compact arm that ended in a thick-fingered blunt hand. His eyes were round, small and watery. They looked as if they were hiding behind the watery film and under the bushy white brows only until the time came to jump out and grab something. He wasn't the sort of man whose pocket you'd try to pick unless you had a lot of confidence in your fingers.

The portrait of Dinah Brand is created against type, in a way unique at the time in this sort of literature. The Op is told that she is tremendously attractive, a de luxe hustler, a woman greedy for money but fatally attractive to men. When he meets Dinah he finds that she has 'the face of a girl of twenty-five already showing signs of wear', with eyes that are large and blue but also bloodshot, a mouth that is big and ripe but has lines at the corners. Her coarse hair needs trimming, her lipstick is uneven, there is a run down the front of one stocking. She is very mean, and a tremendous drinker. Hammett's achievement is to convey the charm and sexual attractiveness of this untidy girl.

Red Harvest is a strongly moral book about civic corruption, and it has a brutality that reflects something in Hammett's own character. There are a good many jokes in the book, but they are all bitter. Any drink Polly de Voto sells you is good, Dinah tells the Op, except maybe the Bourbon. 'That always tastes a little bit like it had been drained off a corpse.' When the Op blackmails Elihu Willsson into acting virtuously by threatening to make public the letters written by the old man to Dinah he says that the letters are hot, and adds: 'I haven't laughed so much over anything since the hogs ate my kid brother.' The Op's own activities become so dubious and so vicious that one of the operatives sent out to work with him thinks that he has killed Dinah, and goes back to San Francisco. It is not surprising that *Roadhouse Nights,* the film said to have been based on *Red Harvest,* retained nothing of the plot and gave no screen credit to Hammett. The dialogue would sound marvellous, but even in the day of Dirty Harry the greed and violence of the characters might be too rough for the screen.

THE ART

After *Red Harvest,* it would seem that Hammett felt there was a limit to what could be achieved by direct accounts of violence, that the same points could and should be made more subtly. His first attempt to do this was the confused and disappointing *The Dain Curse,* with a distinctly softened Op telling the story. *The Maltese Falcon* (*Black Mask* 1929–30, published as a novel in the same year) replaced the Op by Sam Spade, but also took almost all the violence off stage. We are told about people being killed, but don't see it happening.

Hammett's books can be viewed from one point of view as a series of dialogues and confrontations, through which the plot is revealed and tension built up. In *The Maltese Falcon* we begin with Spade and Brigid O'Shaughnessy, and move on to Spade-Dundy, Spade-O'Shaughnessy, Spade-Cairo and so on. Much the same applies to *The Glass Key.* These are stories in which conversation is made to do the work of description, and also of characterisation. We are never in doubt that Gutman and Joel Cairo are villains, but what about Spade himself? 'Don't be too sure I'm as crooked as I'm supposed to be,' he says to Brigid, but he never directly answers her question, when she asks whether he would have gone along with the villains if the falcon had been real. And in *The Glass Key* we are left in doubt about the relationship between Ned Beaumont and Paul Madvig. We can see that Madvig is a crooked politician in the American style, bluff and shrewd but not really too quick in the uptake. Beaumont works for him, protects him by staging a fake quarrel which Madvig believes to be real, later gets beaten up for him, but what is Beaumont's own attitude? Are we to regard him as less corrupt than Madvig, and if so why does he work in Madvig's organisation? To such questions Hammett deliberately returns no answer. Such ambiguities

George Raft in the
original 1935 film version
of *The Glass Key*

are essential to the art with which, in these two books, he
approaches the complexities of guilt and innocence.

They helped him to create a new type of hero-villain, a
character now common enough, but never rendered with the
depth that is brought to the depiction of Spade and Beaumont.
Such a hero-villain was characteristically an American of the
Prohibition era and the depression. He reflected the contradictory feelings of respectable people towards bootleggers and
gangsters. The activities of bootleggers were to be deprecated,
their casualness about human life was horrifying, yet because
the respectable citizen patronised them they were seen as good
fellows, genial and at times even heroic. The events of the
depression, together with the rise of Fascism, encouraged in
the same respectable citizen the belief that the judicious use of
force was the best protection against organised labour.

Like Raymond Chandler later on, Hammett used scenes and
devices from the Op stories in these novels. The clue to
Archer's death, the fact that he let his killer approach close
enough for powder burns to show, comes directly from 'Who
Killed Bob Teal?', and *The Glass Key* is in some ways a
reworking of *Red Harvest,* which in turn owes a good deal to

the story 'Nightmare Town'. But Hammett transformed these scenes and devices in using them again, and did so with remarkably little loss of realism. The problem that he faced was that of reconciling the 'passage from street to paper' of violent scenes from life, with the need to give these scenes the shape of art. He did so first by cutting down overt violence, and then by conveying indirectly the things he wanted to show. Hammett once said to James Thurber that *The Maltese Falcon* had been influenced by Henry James's *The Wings of the Dove,* and although the comparison may seem far-fetched (the central characters in both books are concerned with a fabulous fortune) this does suggest the seriousness with which Hammett approached his work.

He was entirely serious in his masterpiece, *The Glass Key.* The manifold subtleties of this book range from the intricacies of motive already suggested to those of the plot, from the clever crookedness of the hat trick played by Beaumont on Bernie Despain to the deliberate destruction of the publisher Mathews. In this book Hammett also approached for the first time the question of American class relationships. Madvig is a big man in local politics but is still not really acceptable at the Senator's house because he wears silk socks with tweeds. At the same time the Senator needs him, so he gets invited to dinner. Beaumont is acceptable because (although we are never told this in so many words) he knows the social *mores* of the Senator, even though he may not adhere to them.

In these books Hammett pushed outwards the boundaries of the American crime story. Homosexuality was not unknown in such fiction, but it was not a common theme, and Hammett's depiction of the homosexual gunman Wilmer and his relationship with Gutman ('I feel towards Wilmer just exactly as if he were my own son') was very bold. So, of course, was the fact that Spade slept with Brigid. Within the context of the time, Hammett's treatment of sex was extremely frank. The beating-up of Beaumont by the apish Jeff in *The Glass Key,* Jeff's insistence that Beaumont likes it ('I never seen a guy that liked being hit so much or that I liked hitting so much . . . He's a God-damned massacrist, that's what he is'), and the use of Jeff's instinctive sadism by Beaumont in killing Shad O'Rory remain perhaps the most horrific scenes of their kind in any crime story. In *Red Harvest* the Op speaks of getting a rear out of violence, and this is made specific in *The Thin Man,* where Nora asks Nick, after he has tangled with Mimi Jorgensen, 'Tell me the truth: when you were wrestling with Mimi, didn't you have an erection?' The question was omitted from the magazine version of the book, and also from the

English edition. Erections did not at that time exist in the English novel.

The Glass Key is a masterpiece of plotting, but one hopes and believes that Hammett ranked it in a different class from the rest of his books because in it, for the first time, his mastery of technique was truly used for artistic ends. The relationships between the characters, and not just the main characters but those concerning such a minor figure as Opal Madvig, are conveyed with wonderful restraint. In addition the main theme of corruption, social and personal, is handled in a way beyond the reach of any other American novelist of the time. The book can bear comparison with any American novel of the Thirties: it does not look out of place when put beside what Hemingway, Faulkner, Fitzgerald, were writing at the time.

After *The Glass Key* – or so one sees with hindsight – Hammett could go no further with fiction in the form of the crime story. It had become hampering to him, as once it had been a liberation. If he stuck to it now, there was no way he could go but down. And down, sure enough, Hammett went in his last, and immensely popular, book *The Thin Man*.

This was begun in 1930 as a story designed to follow *The Glass Key*. Sixty-five pages were written and then, as Hammett said later, he put the book aside for nearly three years, and then 'found it easier, or at least generally more satisfactory, to keep only the basic idea of the plot'. Apart from the use of the names Guild and Wynant the unfinished typescript, he said, had 'a clear claim to virginity', although some of the incidents were used in the film *After the Thin Man*. I have not read the complete typescript, but it is clear that the characterisation of both Guild and Wynant was on a different and deeper level than anything in the book Hammett eventually produced.

It was written in an interlude between drinking sessions in, Lillian Hellman tells us in her introduction to *The Big Knockover*, a cheap and dismal hotel run by the novelist, Nathanael West. 'Life changed: the drinking stopped, the parties were over. The locking-in time had come and nothing was allowed to disturb it until the book was finished. I had never seen anybody work that way: the care for every word, the pride in the neatness of the typed page itself, the refusal for ten days or two weeks to go out even for a walk for fear something would be lost.' The book that came out was a brilliant piece of work, a sparkling comedy done in terms of a murder mystery, in many places a very funny story. For Hammett, however, it was taking an easy option. He returned to first person narration, which had been given up in the two

William Powell, Myrna Loy
and Asta in the 1934 film
The Thin Man

previous books and the unfinished version of *The Thin Man*. This provided for him, as for Chandler later on, a comfortable ration of wisecracks and side-of-the-mouth comments. Everything is sacrificed to easy, flip reactions and to the relationship of Nick and Nora, which is done very well but necessarily remains superficial because, after all, this is just a comedy. No doubt Hammett deceived himself into thinking that this was an interim book, written between better ones, but if there had ever been a chance of this, the novel's tremendous success made it impossible. *The Thin Man* was the end of a career.

In his twelve years as a writer Dashiell Hammett did a great deal, apart from being the Onlie Begetter of the true American crime story. *The Glass Key* is a magnificent novel, *The Maltese Falcon* remains a model of the detective thriller, no other book of the time gives violence and corruption the raw reality of *Red Harvest*. Almost everything he wrote, after the earliest pieces, was stamped with a personal mark. He was an original writer in style and approach, and there are few of whom one can truly use the word. The least of his work is interesting, the best has a permanent place in literature.

Raymond Chandler.

Chandler and Hammett

GAVIN LYALL: *I think Chandler's done better in England – possibly because he was originally English and educated here, possibly because he presented a slightly more romanticised view of the American underworld (than Hammett). It was almost seen through Hollywood eyes and moreover it came at a time in the 1940's when America was terribly important to us. Chandler was the tuppence coloured version. I don't think he was nearly as accurate about the American cities as Hammett was, but at the time we certainly thought he was.*

From an interview in the *Crime Writers* television series.

Other Hardboiled Heroes

Pulp magazines flourished in the twenties and thirties. Apart from *Black Mask* there were many others, with titles like *Detective Story Magazine, Thrilling Detective, Dime Mystery Clues* or *The Underworld Magazine,* all catering for the almost insatiable demand for tough exciting stories. Most of the magazines and the writers have been forgotten, but *Black Mask* acquired a reputation as something much better than the rest.

This reputation was due to a considerable extent to the editorship of Captain Joseph Shaw. Shaw was appointed editor in 1926, and lost no time in making his intentions clear. He announced in the magazine that the classical detective story inspired by Edgar Allan Poe was dead. He wanted stories where action, emotional tension and character were more important than solutions. New writers like Horace McCoy and

Erle Stanley Gardner joined Carrol John Daly and Hammett in its pages. McCoy went on to write very tough novels, often with social themes, but violence remained an important element. His best book is probably *They Shoot Horses, Don't They?*, a chilling account of the Depression set against the background of a marathon dance contest. Erle Stanley Gardner had a background of many years practising law, and later created the Perry Mason stories, one of the most successful of all courtroom drama series. A prolific and best-selling writer, his books show considerable expert knowledge of law and forensic science.

The success of *Black Mask* also attracted new readers, and among them was Raymond Chandler. The magazine made a great impression on him and he decided to try to write for it. In 1933, at the age of 45, his first short story 'Blackmailers Don't Shoot' was published in *Black Mask*. By this time Hammett had already graduated from pulp magazines to hard covers, and his influence on Chandler was considerable. In a book review in 1931 Dorothy Parker had compared Sam Spade with Sir Launcelot, and it was this knight-errant quality above all that Chandler took from the stories. He idealized the private eye as a romantic figure, a man whom he described in his much-quoted essay 'The Simple Art of Murder' as 'not himself mean, who is

From the film *They Shoot Horses Don't They?* with Jane Fonda and Michael Sarrazin

neither tarnished nor afraid. The detective in this kind of story must be such a man. He is the hero, he is everything. He must be a complete man and a common man and yet an unusual man. He must be, to use a rather weathered phrase, a man of honour, by instinct, by inevitability, without thought of it, and certainly without saying it. He must be the best man in his world and a good enough man for any world.'

This romanticism, combined with Chandler's wit and literary style produced highly individual stories that soon found a popular following, and he followed Hammett in moving from the pulp magazines to hardbacks with *The Big Sleep* which came out in 1939.

Erle Stanley
Gardner

The private eye, first described by Daly, brought to life by Hammett and stylised by Chandler, became a literary convention. In the hands of writers with little talent or originality he is simply a stereotype becoming blurred by constant re-use, but he remains an enduring character of crime fiction. When used by writers of real talent, like Ross Macdonald, the private detective is capable of life and development. In Macdonald's Lew Archer books the detective uncovers not just the criminal, but the roots of the crime which often lie as much as three generations in the past. His portrayals of the corrosive effects of guilt hidden within a family and of the lack of understanding between the generations give his stories a notable degree of compassion.

Edward G. Robinson in the 1930 film *Little Caesar*

Ross Macdonald

The private eye character

GAVIN LYALL: *The basic private eye character, the loner, hasn't himself changed very much except with the tougher language, the tougher actions that are the fashion in the thriller world. I think he's something that's just kept on going through Philip Marlow, through Lew Archer, through hundreds of others in the movies, on the television. I use the character myself in adventure stories . . . basically, one has to admit, that this is the man you're using. He's a literary convention, but he can be real.*

From an interview in the *Crime Writers* television series.

The private detective was not the only product of the hardboiled school that originated in the pulp magazines. The twenties and thirties saw the return of the criminal as hero. Some of Hammett's books have ambiguous heroes, like Sam Spade or Ned Beaumont, but the books of W. R. Burnett have a romantic emphasis on the criminal. *Little Caesar, The Asphalt Jungle* and *High Sierra* all make the criminal the focal point of the story. However inevitable the ultimate triumph of law and order in Burnett's books it is the portraits of the criminals that give them their power. Burnett had considerable knowledge of the world of professional crime, and his books are often close to the kind of story that was making the front page in the newspapers. James M. Cain is another writer who used crime and criminals as the basis of his stories. Unlike Burnett he had little interest in the professional criminal, but wrote about morally weak characters unable to resist temptation. Sex and financial gain are usually interwoven motives, and although the crimes are generally relatively

Chicago in Prohibition days.
(*Above*) The Saint Valentine's Day Massacre in 1929;
(*top right*) soup kitchen run by Al Capone

small scale, the sense of evil and corruption in the stories is strong. His best known books are *The Postman Always Rings Twice* and *Double Indemnity*. Both were made into successful films, the latter directed by Billy Wilder with a screenplay by Chandler. Cain was still producing books well into the nineteen seventies.

The tremendous popularity of the hardboiled school cannot be attributed simply to the talents of the writers. The books and magazines coincided with an emotional climate in tune with the toughness and cynicism expressed in the stories. Prohibition had been introduced in America in January 1920, and whatever effect it had on drinking habits it provided a golden opportunity for crime. Bootlegging soon became big business, and the organisation needed to run a national distribution for alcohol increased the opportunities in all other fields of crime. Corruption of police and politicians became commonplace in the big cities, and known underworld bosses were in more danger from their rivals than from the forces of the law.

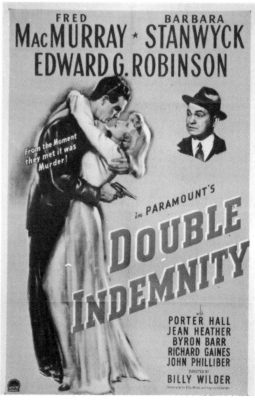

FRED MacMURRAY ★ BARBARA STANWYCK
EDWARD G. ROBINSON

From the Moment they met it was Murder!

in PARAMOUNT'S

DOUBLE INDEMNITY

with
PORTER HALL
JEAN HEATHER
BYRON BARR
RICHARD GAINES
JOHN PHILLIBER
DIRECTED BY
BILLY WILDER

Both detectives and criminals were in different ways in rebellion against established society, a fact emphasised by their lower-class origins. The detective's apparent failure is a mask for his rebellion, his rejection of the material values of society, while on the other hand the criminal hero delights in a display of wealth and possessions but remains aggressively lower class in his attitudes and manners. These qualities had a great appeal for people unemployed or ruined by the depression. For them society had become repressive and corrupt. In *The Long Goodbye* Berni Ohls says 'There ain't no clean way to make a hundred million bucks. . . . Big money is big power and big power gets used wrong. It's the system'. His words expressed the feelings of people who had lost faith in society.

The books of the hardboiled writers, particularly Burnett, Chandler and Hammett, were very influential in the development of the American cinema. The tight, economical storytelling, the revelation of character by action, the naturalism of the dialogue and the toughness of the humour – all these qualities were ideal for the cinema. The films based on books by these writers include some of the finest of the period, though as the director, Billy Wilder, observed, the lesser books often made the better films.

Through the cinema the books reached a wider audience, even though this was at second hand. Both the detective and the gangster were heroes, and the ambiguity of their appeal can be seen by the frequent use of the same actors for both types of role. The best example is Humphrey Bogart, who played the detective in *The Maltese Falcon* and *The Big Sleep*, and with equal success the hunted criminal in *High Sierra*. The appeal of the books is so lasting that new film adaptations continue to appear. There have been recent remakes of Chandler's *The Long Goodbye*, *Farewell my Lovely* and *The Big Sleep,* and *Private Eye,* an adaptation of Hammett's *The Dain Curse* stories starring James Coburn.

While the hardboiled writers were changing the face of American crime fiction a different development was taking place in Europe. In 1931 Georges Simenon published his first eleven Maigret novels. He became the first French language crime writer since Gaboriau to achieve international popularity.

(*Left*) Chandler, the scriptwriter

Humphrey Bogart
in three classic
roles on either side
of the law. (*Top*)
as Sam Spade in
The Maltese Falcon
with Mary Astor;
(*centre*) as Philip
Marlowe in
The Big Sleep with
Lauren Bacall;
(*bottom*) as the
wanted criminal in
High Sierra with
Ida Lupino

5
Simenon and Highsmith: Into the criminal's head

by Maurice Richardson

'To set up what you like against what you dislike. This is the disorder of the mind' . . . That was one of the sayings of Seng-T's An, the Third Zen Buddhist Patriarch. I always associate it with the reply of Count Mippipopolous, the Greek bon viveur in Hemingway's *Fiesta,* when Jake said he ought to write a book about wines. 'Mr Barnes, all I want out of wines is to enjoy them . . .' Is this the way to begin a critical exercise? Is it not veering towards the quasi-mystical attitude of many readers of crime fiction, the kind that are called, and often playfully call themselves addicts, those for whom we say the detective story is the opium of the middle-classes? Yet even among these the discriminatory faculty exists. I once heard a fierce argument between an ambassador and his wife about a single sentence in a new Edgar Wallace, that had just been flown out in the diplomatic bag: 'In the room was an iron bed which was made.' The ambassador said it was incomprehensible and slipshod and Edgar Wallace ought to have his dictaphone taken away. The ambassadress said not at all; it was a first class piece of up-to-date monosyllabic colloquial prose worthy of Gertrude Stein . . .

Fortunately, there is no need to set up Simenon against Highsmith because they are like claret and burgundy, and if asked which I prefer, I can only answer both. And both are excellent if not indeed the outstanding examples of modern crime-writers whose novels are automatically treated as not only entertaining – and all stories, whether tragic or comic, are supposed to entertain – but as serious contributions to

literature. Simenon has been compared by Gide, Mauriac, Raymond Mortimer and others to Balzac. It is almost impossible to refrain from attaching the label genius to him. And the late Francis Hope, a most fastidious literary intellectual, former Fellow of All Souls, who perished, sadly young, in an air crash, remarked, after reading her eleventh novel, *Those Who Walk Away,* that if there was a contemporary crime writer who could possibly be encountered in the same street as Dostoevsky, it was Patricia Highsmith. So I do not need to waste anybody's time on shades of distinction between high, middle and low crime-writing.

We bracket Simenon and Highsmith together as 'psychological' crime-writers because they are both preoccupied with motivation, and because they both go in for putting their characters in stress situations, and then letting them reveal their true, and often psychopathological, nature. I must admit, however that I never really quite know what precisely is meant by a psychological crime novel, though I must have used the expression scores of times. I suppose Dostoevsky's *Crime And Punishment* is the paradigm here. I can tell you which the prototypical psychoanalytical detective-story is, of course. It is Oedipus, in which the detective finds out that he himself has done it. In recent times the nearest approach to this, as Dr Charles Rycroft, the psychoanalyst, has pointed out, is Wilkie Collins' *The Moonstone,* in which the hero, Franklin Blake, in a sleep-walking trance under the influence of opium, steals the diamond . . . But this is just something for you to ruminate over. It is time to consider our authors separately. I will begin with Simenon.

His real name is Georges Sim. He is Belgian, born in Liège, in 1903, of petit-bourgeois parents, mother Flemish, father Walloon. Although he has lived in France for much of his life and appears to have any amount of Gallic esprit, he is really far more Belgian than French. There is a distinct tincture of Flemish gloom in his make-up. Psychiatrists have suggested that his vast productivity is a kind of manic pressure activity, a continuous escape from melancholy. This may seem to be the kind of snap diagnosis psychiatrists are apt to make on insufficient evidence. Yet there is no doubt that his Belgian background, in which he is deeply rooted, nearly always figures as sombre in the extreme. You get the impression of a continuum of wet Sundays. There is a special kind of rain, 'black rain,' (the title of one of his books) which has come to be associated with Simenon.

At 16 he was a reporter on the *Gazette de Liège*. At 17 he wrote his first novel. At 20 he married his first wife – he's had two or three since – and moved to Paris. There he met Colette and she taught him how to write, and above all to cut. She used to send his exercises back time and again until sometimes he thought they were going to fade away, into white space. It was largely thanks to her that he developed his clipped laconic style, in which what has been omitted can sometimes be almost as important as what is said. Between 1923 and 1933 he published 200 different novels under 16 different pseudonyms. He lived mostly in his yacht, the Ostrogot, cruising about the canals and rivers of France; the Mediterranean; the Black Sea, where he took a quick and dim view of Stalin's Russia later reflected in *The Window Over The Way;* and the Baltic, where he wrote the first of the Maigret novels. For two years he wrote one Maigret book a month. In 1933 he took a rest from Maigret for a bit, and wrote 'straight' novels, most of them psychological studies of criminal or violent actions and passions.

After the war he lived in America, mainly in Arizona, for a few years. It didn't really suit him, and the novels he wrote about the American scene, including an essay in gangsterism, *The Brothers Rico,* are not his best.

Smallish but muscular, Simenon is an athletic type; there is little of the intellectual about him, though he is a widely read man. He rides, plays golf and bridge, and chases girls. He has various little quirks that are good value for gossip columnists: his innumerable pipes; the solid gold ball he keeps tossing in the air, a sort of worry-bead substitute; his sudden almost embarrassing outbursts of sexual frankness – or is it megalomania? – about the legion of his mistresses. His personality is elusive.

When I met him in London after the war I got the impression he was an actor playing the role that was expected of him. He wore a very smart brown suit, but with it a large weird floppy lilac bow-tie that suggested a teacher at a *lycée*. He was very amiable and polite and launched at once into a conventional old-fashioned spiel about how he adored your London with its fogs and how much he owed to 'your great Dickens'. He was a very efficient publicity agent. (He handles all his affairs himself, never uses an agent.) When I told him how good I thought *The Man Who Watched The Trains Go By* was, he shrugged his shoulders. 'Oh that. The French medical schools have recommended it to students of psychiatry as a better study of paranoia than any text book.'

I asked him how he wrote. Once the period of gestation was

over, he said, and he had decided to begin a new book, it was all done in two hours' work, early each morning. He sat down at his typewriter, paused for a few minutes to get into a kind of trance-like state . . . 'et alors je tape.' And so, at a rate of 20 quarto pages in two hours, the day's work at the conscious level was done. That's what he said, anyway.

Apart from the 200 pseudonymous preliminary canters, he has written 212 novels, 80 of them about Maigret, been translated into 42 languages and published in 32 countries. There have been human fiction-factories before, but not of his quality of output. Edgar Wallace dictated a 70,000-word novel in a weekend. A veteran Amalgamated Press hack, one of the Frank Richards brigade, sitting in dressing-gown, shawl, and skull-cap behind a battered Underwood at a roll-top desk in his Edwardian villa at Twickenham, was still turning out 10,000 words of office-boys serial per day when close on 80. But you can't compare them with Simenon. I suppose Trollope, with his steady 3,000 words, every morning between 5.50 and 8.30, is the nearest equivalent.

It was some little time before Simenon caught on outside France. Two of his books, *The Yellow Dog* and *The Disintegration Of J.P.G.* – a very clever typically oblique story of a little schoolmaster who comes under the spell of a set of louche characters and falls apart – were published in England and America in the mid thirties. They didn't sell because they were half the length of the average novel, and the Anglo-Saxon book trade in those days was as rigid in its conventions as a Rotary Club. Then, in 1939, T. M. Ragge, of Routledge, had the bright idea of publishing two Maigret novels together in one volume at 8s. 6d. It became a best seller despite the war and the compulsively readable Simenon was launched in the English speaking world on a flood tide.

Inspector Maigret of the Police Judicaire is a strange mixture of the conventional and unconventional. He is a powerful character and much rounder than his numerous counterparts at Scotland Yard or the Police Precincts of New York and Los Angeles. He looms up at you in his bowler hat and heavy overcoat, with globules of mist clinging to its nap, and you feel you can touch him. His frequent pauses in cafés for white wine, calvados or even, in a crisis, pernod, generate for English readers a delicious sensation of touristic nostalgia very different from the non-kick you get when Inspector Tibbets samples British Railways beer at Liverpool Street while waiting for his train to Gidea Park.

Maigret's most fervent admirers will tell you he is not so much a character as a myth, symbolising Justice and every-

Three television Maigrets
with their creator
(*Left to right*) Jan Teulings,
Simenon, Gino Cervi and
Rupert Davies

thing that is best in the French bourgeoisie. It wasn't his fault
that France collapsed in 1940. You wouldn't have thought he
had an enemy, apart from criminals, but after the liberation
the communist poet Aragon was darting his forked tongue all
over Paris telling everyone that the model for Maigret was an
archcollaborator. However, Maigret, as created by Simenon is
indisputably benevolent. Today some of the younger generation, to whom police corruption, via American crime fiction
and British newspapers, has become a commonplace, find
Maigret a little too good to be true. Why, they complain, do we
never see him taking a bit of dropsy from the boys? Why does
he always trot off home to that old bag, Madame Maigret, and
her tripe and rabbit casserole, instead of dropping into a
brothel and having a bird on the house?

Myself I never question Maigret's integrity, and it helps to
sustain his role as a catalytic agent who touches off a
psychological reaction in the criminal that often ends in the
criminal giving himself away. Simenon, who is a master of
implication, also conjures up for you the squalid side of police
work, with its interpenetration of cops and crooks, and the
ubiquitous informers. The waiting game, which Maigret plays
rather than active investigation, is one of his most distinctive
features. Another is the lifelike casual, almost throwaway
nature of Simenon's plots. He eschews planted red-herrings or
artificial tricks to heighten suspense. And although, in most of
his stories, the murderer is unknown to start with, he never
manipulates the action so as to produce that last minute

showdown with the stunning surprise finish. And his laconic, elided style, combining cinematic vividness, due to choice of the significant detail, with the austerity of a précis-writer, gives you a strong sense of motion and change. You never feel you want to tell him to get on with it. He is cunning, too, at making a relatively flat piece of dialogue sound characteristic. The result is an exceptionally strong feeling of verisimilitude, that 'this-is-it' feeling.

I think, however, it must be remembered that Maigret is essentially a nineteen-thirties figure. He belongs to Paris before the war, and so do all the Maigret stories that Simenon has written since. I do not know that this matters very much, though Taine, with his insistence on 'le moment' would probably have attached some importance to it. But I am convinced that the pre-war Maigret books are the best. (Thomas Narcejac, himself a French writer of psychological thrillers, takes the opposite view in his *The Art of Simenon.*) There are two stories that, if pressed, I would single out from all the rest. They are *A Battle Of Nerves* and *Liberty Bar,* both published in France in 1932.

In *A Battle Of Nerves,* Maigret plays his most extreme waiting game with a psychopathic red-haired Czech medical student, who might almost have come from Dostoevsky's *The Possessed.* He has murdered a rich American woman and thinks the police have got nothing on him. Day after day, Maigret sits it out with him in the Rotonde in Montparnasse until eventually the young man, though too tough to crack, acts in a way that gives the game away. In *Liberty Bar* the unforgettable character is Ja Ja, an enormously fat tart who keeps a bar in Cannes. She was infatuated with an American alcoholic, who has been murdered. How she came to do it – for it is soon fairly obvious that she did – through what blend of injured vanity and aggression suddenly mobilised, is revealed almost light-heartedly in the course of conversation. You might say that while Maigret's professional attitude towards his customers is one of compassionate determinism, Simenon's towards his characters is one of determinist compassion.

Of course he can't be expected always to keep up the same high level. Yet it is extraordinary how seldom he ever lets you down. I have read scores of Maigrets written between the thirties and the late sixties and I cannot think of one of them that has been a really serious disappointment. You might think that the inevitable repetition, especially in some of the later ones, when Maigret seems to rely more on his aides in the official setting, made extra-familiar by the BBC TV series, would pall. And sometimes one does begin with a sinking feeling of 'Oh Lord, not again!' only to be seduced by the sharp tangy atmosphere, whether the setting is Paris, or the Provinces or the Seine and its tributaries with their amphibious riparian inhabitants – a favourite environment this, where the characters vary from bargees and down-and-outs to a raffish English retired Anglo-Indian colonel, a vicious old alcoholic somewhat optimistically described as a Milord. *Maigret And The Young Girl, Maigret's Mistake, Maigret Stonewalled, Maigret's Revolver, Maigret And the Hundred Gibbets, Maigret And the Flea, Maigret And the Old Lady, Maigret in London* . . . but this is ridiculous; there's 80 of them.

The mood of the majority of Simenon's 132 straight novels is sombre. There is seldom anyone to diffuse those patches of mild euphoria that Maigret can impart when he is sipping and smoking and sniffing 'that smell which was for him the very quintessence of a Parisian morning; the smell of cafe crème and hot croissants with a dash of rum'.

The novels' subjects vary from the fortunes of the Donadieu family of Nantes, with whom he has one of his quasi-Balzacian obsessions, to abrupt tours de force, short sharp chronicles that might almost be photostats of pages from the Recording Angel's ledger. His longest novel is *Pedigree* (1948) a haunting chronicle of childhood and adolescence in Liège, before and during the first world war. It is based on his own youth and some say it tells you more about Simenon himself than his autobiography. It also contains the germs of many of the characters of other novels, both earlier and later, particularly some of his Dostoevskyan psychopaths, like the Czech in *The Patience Of Maigret,* and the wild boy who murders his employer in *Magnet Of Doom*. But very few of his novels belong to the genre of scrambled autobiography. His inventive power is very strong and he doesn't need much to touch it off; a chance encounter, a quick passing glimpse, *faits divers* in the press may be enough to start him story-telling. And he has a keen feeling for the genius loci.

The style of Simenon's straight novels is not noticeably different from that of the Maigret cycle; it is more a matter of mood. Once having absorbed Colette's lessons, he proceeded to short-circuit, as one critic has put it, 'the not always advantageous innovations that symbolism and Americanism have contributed to French prose. His affinities are rather with 19th century realists: de Maupassant; and perhaps even Zola,' though in a much streamlined version. He seldom goes in for fine writing, though it is noticeable that when a character is ruminating over his past, especially if it is Belgian, the syntax becomes charged with emotion. His descriptions have a direct,

Jean Gabin portrayed many Simenon heroes. He is seen here with Brigitte Bardot in *Love is my Profession (En cas de malheur)*

physical quality. He can simplify his scenes, using primary colours like a painter of the Naif school and he has a wonderful eye for the single significant detail that will act as a peg on which to hang a cloak of atmosphere.

One of Simenon's specialities is portraying ghastly characters and atrocious actions, dispassionately, with complete objectivity, so that the reader feels the behaviour is inevitable and shares the Simenonian attitude of: 'Judge not, lest ye be judged.' There is never a trace of sentimentality; Simenon is an empathiser rather than a sympathiser. Again and again he brings off these strange moral coups without ever moralising. One example from his post-war period is *Striptease* in which Celita, a dancer in a tatty little Riviera night club, and offical mistress of the proprietor, becomes insanely jealous of the new girl, Maud, whose gaucherie enables her to strip as it were artlessly, with a sensational air of innocence. Trust Simenon to know what will prove to be the nodal point in a stripteaser's life. Celita's spitefulness is literally fiendish, the kind that used to be attributed to witches. Yet it has the effect of making you feel frightened, not of her but for her; and her abrupt

Still from the film
The Stain on the Snow
(La Neige était sale)
with Daniel Gelin as
Frank Friedmaier

suicide, due to a sudden backfire of aggression is a natural culmination. It is one of his slighter stories but it stays with you.

Perhaps the champion monster of all his stories is Frank Friedmaier in *The Stain on the Snow*. This is a strange novel, the only one, almost, that Simenon wrote about the German occupation, though it is set in a slight haze of equivocation, as if time had telescoped, and you can't be absolutely certain whether you are in the first world war or the second. Some of Simenon's admirers will tell you this gives an effect of greater depth. Personally I like to know precisely what time it is as well as exactly where I am. The last war was rather a sore subject with Simenon and perhaps that was why he put a veil over it. But there is nothing in the least equivocal about Frank's behaviour. He is the illegitimate son of a procuress in a large unspecified Belgian town and he is a thief, a ponce, a sadist, and a gratuitous murderer; he takes perverse delight in procuring his own girl for another man. A Freudian might call him a criminal whose super-ego or conscience works in reverse gear. Then, quite suddenly, when arrested by the Germans, he experiences an inner crisis, in relation to the parental figure of the girl's father, and behaves with great courage, refusing to talk under torture and going to his death like a man. One accepts him in both phases almost as readily as one accepts some of Dostoevsky's young nihilists.

What one would like is a carefully selected edition of his best – say twenty – books, though it might be difficult to reach agreement. Everyone has their favourites. One of my own is *Banana Tourist* (1938) set in Tahiti where Simenon stayed a month and then caught the next boat back. 'Touriste de Banane' was then the local name for the romantic young bums who landed on the island, broke, and expected the fruit to drop into their mouths. Simenon's banana tourist is a sad young man, a connection of the Donadieu family, a melancholic idealist. He arrives, typically, in a torrential downpour that lasts for three days. This is not a mere debunking-Tahiti device, for the bright colours of the island are accentuated when the sun comes out, but the mood has been set. The little waterfront hotel where he stays in Papeete, kept by a tough provencale, frequented by Tahitian tarts, whose friendly casualness only accentuates his loneliness, and minor French colonial officials, is wonderfully real. So is the coastal village where he dives into the bush and gets bitten by ticks and half-starves until rescued by order of the authorities. His suicide back in the hotel, in the bed where he has just been sleeping with one of the girls, is a matter for shoulder shrugging. There is something highly original about the way in which Simenon uses the melancholy mood here to give a traditionally exotic scene the sharpest kind of everyday circumstantial reality.

Though in general a non-political animal, Simenon has written his way into the political area now and then. *The Premier* is a case in point. This is a study of an 82-year-old ex-Prime Minister who has retired to a villa on the Normandy cliffs. He has had one stroke but remains as lively as a fly. (He is popularly supposed to have been to some extent modelled on Clemenceau.) France is in one of its periodical governmental crises and Charlemont, who was once the Premier's secretary, has been asked to form a cabinet. But tucked away in one of his books the Premier has a confession signed by Charlemont of how he betrayed government devaluation secrets to a bank. Half dozing, the old man recaps about this and about his own past, including the great scandal when, as a young junior minister, he was caught having his patroness's social secretary on the sofa. At the end past and present are neatly linked up. This is Simenon at his most human.

Patricia Highsmith – Mary Patricia Highsmith, though nobody would dream of using her first Christian name – was born in Fort Worth, Texas, in 1921. Her birthday falls on the same day, 19th February, as Edgar Allan Poe's, towards whom she has sometimes been credited with a certain neo-Gothic affinity. She has Scottish, German, and English in her pedigree, and looks as if it might have collected a dash of red Indian somewhere along the line; she rather hopes it has. Both her parents were commercial artists. Her father's name was Plangman, but he and her mother separated four months before she was born and she took the name of her step-father. She didn't meet her real father until she was twelve. He put his hand on the table beside hers and she saw that their hands were exactly the same shape, strong square and practical; she is an excellent carpenter and a by no means negligible painter.

She went to school in New York, wrote comic superman stories after graduating from Columbia University, was turned down for a job with *Vogue* because she looked too farouche and had never owned a hat. She has a passion for animals, most especially cats. She keeps snails, those interesting significant hermaphrodites, and takes a scientific interest in their behaviour. A recent book of her short stories *Beastly Murder*, in which various species take their revenge on the human race, suggests almost a pananimalian ideology. Though outwardly friendly enough towards the human race, she is a congenital loner and admits that she is simply isn't capable of 'togetherness'.

For the past ten years she has been living in France near Fontainebleau. Before that she lived in a Suffolk village and before that in Italy and Mexico. But her basic American-ness is very evident, unaltered by cosmopolitanism. She is apt to be diffident, but is natural and downright. Work is probably her ruling passion and she is inclined to be obsessional about it. An American woman journalist who interviewed her in 1977, came away with the impression that, despite her age, of 56, she was in some ways curiously reminiscent of a college-girl.

At present Miss Highsmith, after a traumatic publishing experience, is riding the crest of a wave. Her last book, *Edith's Diary* (1977), which was a piece of straight rather than crime-fiction, was first turned down by the American publisher to whom she was under contract. But when it did come out it got rave notices on both sides of the Atlantic, and established her as a cult figure on the Continent. In 1978, two films and a play based her novels, were running simultaneously. Critics are apt to to get worked up over the sinister atmosphere in her books. Graham Greene, a great admirer of

her as well as of Simenon, wrote in his introduction to *Eleven*, her book of short stories, that she 'creates a world of her own, a world claustrophobic which we enter each time with a sense of personal danger'. I myself am quoted, quite correctly, as saying that 'Miss Highsmith writes about men like a spider writing about flies'. Another reviewer has maintained that 'reading one of her novels is like having tea with a dangerous witch'. It is certainly true that in most of her books things have a habit of going wrong in a seemingly natural sort of way.

Miss Highsmith got off to an almost dangerously high-flying start in 1949. After jettisoning an immensely long novel unfinished, she wrote *Strangers On A Train,* the plot of which she had been nursing for four years. It depends on a fantasy that is not uncommon. Actually, it had been used once before, though not to anything like such good effect, by G.D.H. and Margaret Cole. What happens is that A, who would like to be disembarrassed of an inconvenient relation, meets B, who is in the same predicament. A says he will knock off B's nuisance and there will be no conceivable motive to connect him with the murder, and B will oblige him by performing a similar service. In Highsmith's novel A is Bruno, a brilliant piece of characterisation, a rich garrulous mother-fixated near-alcoholic queer, who wants to be rid of his millionaire father. He dominates his muddle-headed young tennis-playing partner in crime, Guy, as indeed he dominates the entire book. Guy wants to be free of his wife who refuses to give him a divorce

113

but he doesn't take the pact quite seriously until he discovers that Bruno has already carried out his side of the bargain, and expects him to carry out his. The suspense proceeds in zig-zags like a temperature chart, but there is no forced sensationalism. Hitchcock bought the book for a song and made what is generally considered to be his best film out of it.

It was obvious that a new talent had arrived, though *Strangers On A Train* was going to be a difficult novel to live up to. Miss Highsmith has none of Simenon's daemonic facility. She writes and rewrites slowly and carefully in an easy-to-read colloquial matter-of-fact style, spinning away like a Norn. The successor to *Strangers On A Train* was *The Blunderer,* which is rather like its mirror image. In this case A and B have never met. A is once again a strong clever man. He commits a murder and gets away with it. B, weak and silly, is so impressed by A's impeccably fool-proof technique that he tries to imitate it and lands them both in the cart.

Again and again she returns to the theme of a pathological conflict between two men. One of them generally acts seemingly on impulse, as if out of character, as if some tiny little cerebral implosion had taken place. Then he is done for. One of her best novels on these lines is *Deep Water.* The setting is an ordinary prosperous American middle-class commuters community. Victor Van Allen, when we meet him, is drinking whisky and watching his wife dance, but the very first paragraph is a danger signal:

Vic didn't dance, but not for the reasons that most men who don't dance give to themselves. His rationalisation of his attitude was a flimsy one and didn't fool him for a minute, though it crossed his mind every time he saw Melinda dancing. She made dancing embarrassing.

And by the time Melinda takes up with a new boyfriend, Charley de Lisle, a night club pianist, Vic's simmering paranoia is ready to boil. At a summer evening party, by the Cowans' swimming pool, with no risk of being found out, he holds Charley under and drowns him. Melinda thinks he's done it. The situation between them becomes increasingly impossible. Almost more by accident than design, Vic kills another of Melinda's men friends and cracks up altogether. Nothing is concealed or withheld from the reader. It is a perfectly straightfoward account of a man running amok under stress. Put badly like that, it may sound far-fetched, but as told it is completely convincing. (*The Cry Of The Owl* has a similar theme.) An interesting psychological feature is the peculiar quality of Vic's paranoid jealousy with its suggestion of hidden depths, running true to psychiatric text-book form.

Alain Delon as Ripley in
René Clement's film
Purple Noon (Plein Soleil)
made from *The Talented
Mr Ripley*

One of her most interesting novels, which shows her
handling an all-male scene with an easy unforced naturalism,
is *The Glass Cell* (1964). This is a study of Philip, a successful
engineer against whom the dice have been almost too heavily
loaded, reducing him to a cypher. Found guilty of a fraud of
which he was innocent, and sentenced to six years he sits in his
cell thinking about his wife Hazel and what she might be
getting up to. 'He felt in fact like nothing at all, and somehow
like no-one, as if something, some mysterious Parcaean
shears, had cut his tie even to Hazel.' It's a very tough prison,
and a sadistic guard frames him for trafficking in cigarettes
and hangs him up by the thumbs. Afterwards, in hospital, he is
given too much morphine by an eccentric prison doctor, and he
becomes an addict. His character degenerates rapidly and in a
prison riot, touched off by a dispute over a dog, he gratuitu-
ously stamps on a man and kills him. The visits of his pretty
wife only exacerbate his paranoid jealousy. When he comes out
on parole, he goes from bad to worse. He kills two men, one his
lawyer with whom his wife has been having an intermittent
affair, the other the agent of a shady businessman who has

115

been feeding him with exaggerated information about his wife's goings-on. He ends up back in prison again. The prison half of the book is extraordinarily good. I can't think of any male American tough realistic thriller writer (with the possible exception of the neglected W. R. Burnett) who could have done it as well. Miss Highsmith got much of her background material from corresponding with one of her fans, a convict serving a long sentence.

Another study of a paranoid, almost schizophrenic crack-up is *This Sweet Sickness.* This has a plot like madman's fly-trap, but surroundings, settings and subsidiary characters, are so verisimilitudinously matter-of-fact that you don't question it. David, a brilliant young chemist living in a New York boarding house, has a strange week-end fantasy life caring for an entirely nonexistent invalid in a house in the commuter belt, which he has rented under an alias, and into which he has hopes of one day installing his former girl-friend, Annabelle, unhappily married to Gerald, but with whom he is now busily corresponding. He meets Gerald and after a couple of rows, he bashes him and tries to pin it on his own alias. After this he runs amok and ends in a semi-suicidal defenestration. You will hardly believe how well it reads. Disintegration of character and an ambivalent relationship between two men is also the basic theme of *Two Faces Of January,* which has an admirably vivid touristic setting in Greece.

Miss Highsmith is a Queen of Paranoia, whether inherent or induced. This persecution of men by each other is almost as obsessional with her as work itself. It reappears in *The Barbarians,* an excellent short story about an architect who is

Dennis Hopper as Ripley in Wim Wenders' film *The American Friend,* based on *Ripley's Game*

Weston Gavin as Ripley from the *Crime Writers* series

exasperated by noisy louts playing outside his flat. He drops a brick on the head of one of them but only maims him slightly. They know he's done it and he knows they know . . . No doubt the paranoid theme has some inner significance, but it is idle to speculate what writers would be like without their fixation, as Miss Highsmith has remarked herself in a short book she wrote *Plotting And Writing Suspense Fiction*. This is typically matter of fact and sensible, rather like a manual of carpentry, but quite entertaining.

Next to *Strangers On A Train,* her most popular novel has been *The Talented Mr Ripley*. This is a cleverly plotted study of a young American criminal psychopath of great personal charm, and so utterly without any shred of conscience that his crimes seem almost graceful, like the swinging antics of a gibbon in the jungle. Ripley murders a rich friend in Italy and impersonates him and manages to get away with it. He reappears in *Ripley Underground* and again in *Ripley's Game*. In *Ripley Underground,* he has now married a rich French girl and is living in luxury near Fontainebleau. Then his friends in London send him an SOS. The art racket they've all been running, pretending the painter, Derwatt, is still alive, while they turn out a faithful series of imitations of his work which now fetches high prices, is in danger of being rumbled. Ripley helps them out by impersonating Derwatt at an exhibition. Later, in his cellar at Fontainebleau, he brains a suspicious American collector with a bottle of claret. The book ends in the air with the police closing in.

Ripley's Game though readable enough, is the nearest Miss Highsmith has ever got to a conventional thriller. She paused for a while after finishing it, then went to the opposite pole of the straight novel with *Edith's Diary,* which contains no crime to speak of, apart from what has been called 'a minor act of euthanasia'. What she will write next is anybody's guess. She has a powerful original talent and it shows no signs of flagging.

Further Reading

Thomas Narcejac: *The Art of Simenon* (Routledge and Kegan Paul, 1952). This is a very impressionistic appreciation, full of intuitive judgements and typically Gallic generalisations. It can be recommended, with reservations, for its enthusiasm. Its bibliography is incomplete.

John Raymond: *Simenon in Court* (Hamish Hamilton, 1968). Also enthusiastic, of course, but it contains more biographical information as well as a balanced critique.

Crooks and Cops

Lee Marvin in the film *Point Blank*

Patricia Highsmith's presentation of her criminal hero Tom Ripley is unique. No justification or excuse is offered for his actions, he is under neither psychological nor social pressure to commit his crimes, but is motivated only by self interest and is entirely without conscience. Other writers have used a criminal as the protagonist in their stories, but not with such a deliberate reversal of morality.

Richard Stark is the author of fast-moving and violent books featuring a professional criminal named Parker. A lone operator, Parker is often in conflict with the large and powerful organisations that dominate crime in America. Within the confines of the criminal world Parker has his own set of values, and will keep to them even when this places him in considerable danger. He is far closer to the conventional hero than Ripley,

and is in many ways a private eye manqué. In one of Stark's best known books, *Point Blank,* he fights an organisation resembling the Mafia, a nationwide multi-million dollar criminal syndicate, with extensive, legitimate business interests, which almost becomes a distorted image of society. Ted Lewis is a British writer working

(Below) Ted Lewis and (*right*) a scene from the film of his book *Get Carter* with Michael Caine

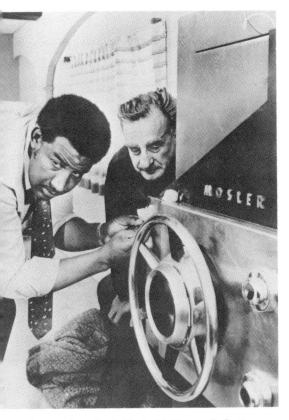

along similar lines with his Carter books. The British setting gives the books a much lower key, for although the criminals may be as ruthless and vicious, the crime is essentially a small-scale local affair. In *Get Carter* other criminals are shown as more corrupt and immoral than Carter, thus helping to justify his murderous campaign against them.

The criminal hero is not always taken seriously. Indeed Donald Westlake (the real name of Richard Stark) has written many comic novels about criminals, like *The Bank Shot* and *The Hot Rock*. The humour is largely based on the idea of the potential criminals being too incompetent to carry out their often elaborate plans. Many other writers have taken up the criminal hero, and the books range from the brutality of Hugh C. Rae's *Skinner* to the wit and sophistication of Kyril Bonfiglioli's *Don't Point That Thing At Me*.

This rise of the criminal hero was accompanied by a new look at the police. Simenon's Inspector Maigret books had already shown that it was possible to make an ordinary, unexciting policeman an interesting character. Maigret performs no stunning feats of logic or deduction, nor does he burst through doors gun in hand. Instead a sympathetic attitude allows him to understand, and even almost to identify with, the suspects. Nicolas Freeling's Van der Valk is

A scene from *Bank Shot* with George C. Scott

Donald E. Westlake

Nicolas Freeling

in many ways similar to Maigret, but the stories have a different quality. Although Van der Valk is a conscientious police officer he is often in conflict with his superiors, and he has a determination to follow the dictates of his own conscience that has something of the private-eye tradition. The characters in the books, including Van der Valk himself, have private lives that exist independently of the criminal investigations, and the books are often as concerned with the roots of crime and the nature of society as with crime itself.

The sympathetic policeman is capable of as many variations as the criminal hero, and a particularly enjoyable one is H. R. F. Keating's Inspector Ghote. Set in Bombay the books are both exotic and humorous, and Inspector Ghote is more than sympathetic, he is very likeable. Often scared of his superiors, Ghote finds himself forced to disobey them if his reason or his heart tell him to, even if this takes him to the brink of disaster. Many of the Ghote books were written before Keating had visited India, and this underlines what all books in this type of police story have in common. They are about imaginary policemen who are not, and probably could not be, part of any real police force. They are an image of the police, but not a picture of the way real policemen work.

Novels dealing with realistic police procedures started to appear in the fifties. One of the first really successful American books was Hillary Waugh's *Last Seen Wearing,* published in 1952. Waugh makes excellent use of the slow routine of police work, the checking and rechecking of all information and the following up of the many, often false, trails. By contrasting this work with the emotions and anxiety of the characters involved he gives a dramatic feeling to the most routine tasks.

In England in 1955 John Creasey wrote the first of his Gideon of the Yard books, using the pseudonym J. J. Marric. In them he conveys much of the feeling of pressure and routine by the now familiar device of running several stories in parallel. The books show real knowledge of policework, although Creasey's admiration for the police excludes any criticism.

Barry Foster as Van der Valk in the television series

(*Above*) Ed McBain and (*right*) some of the *87th Precinct* cops from the television series

Evan Hunter, under the name of Ed McBain, started to write his 87th Precinct series in America in 1956. McBain often uses the device of parallel stories, but he creates the feeling of the police force as a group by not having a single hero in his books. Steve Carella is the main character but the other detectives all play important parts.

Chester Himes

Jack Webb

There are also detailed descriptions of police routine, sometimes involving very gruesome forensic work, that give a feeling of considerable realism in areas which many writers had previously ignored.

The books of Chester Himes are different from the mainstream of police fiction because of the picture they give of a particular people and place. Black himself, Himes writes stories set in Harlem with two black policemen as main characters. His books have a vitality and freshness and give an impression of life in Harlem that manages to be both horrifyingly violent and extremely funny. Himes' macabre sense of humour is illustrated by his bizarre choice of names for his detectives, Grave Digger Jones and Coffin Ed Johnson.

Police fiction on television, starting with Jack Webb's *Dragnet*, instantly became popular. It suited the small screen with its demand for characters who could appear week after week in a wide variety of stories.

6
Four of a kind?

by Troy Kennedy Martin

Dixon, Barlow, Regan and Pyle . . . popular television drama for the last twenty years has been dominated by policemen and police series. There are several reasons for this. From the point of view of the broadcaster, police series have been safe and predictable, a marriage of documentary and *policier* traditions combining information with entertainment. There was something of a public service about them.

However from the point of view of a predominantly working-class audience, the police series was something new in that for the first time they were presented with working class heroes. Up to that time the mass audience had to be content with a diet of Wolsey Films where the Flying Squad were led by public schoolboys.

Furthermore, beginning with Dixon, police series used the policeman as a vehicle to get inside contemporary society. Indeed such was the success of this particular approach that by the early days of *Z Cars,* subject matter which up to that time had been thought the province of TV plays had become preempted by the series. Part of the reason for this take-over was the limitations of the naturalist tradition of TV drama. Information describing the main characters, who they were and what they were up to was filtered through a series of conversations at the opening of the play. This took such a time to pick up, that the beginning of these plays always tended to be slow. However in the police series, where the principal protagonists were already well known the story would start on page one rather than on page ten.

Twenty years after 'Four of a Kind', the first *Z Cars* story, police series have become potentially subversive. The very documentary traditions which were proudly attached to *Z Cars* and *Softly Softly* now demand that they reflect truths (like instances of police corruption and racism) which broadcasters often feel the public may find unpalatable.

When reproached about the lack of commitment to airing these subjects in series the immediate defence of the programme makers is that this sort of stuff is not entertainment, it's boring. 'We have a responsibility to our viewers.' 'These things should be the subject of plays etc.' There is a great deal of truth in this defence but at the same time, on other platforms, the same programme makers don't protest when their products are referred to as realistic. Accepting prizes, they conveniently forget that vast chunks of the police behaviour are out of bounds.

Realism is the critical word most used in relation to police series. Ever since the film of *The Blue Lamp* – the progenitor of *Dixon of Dock Green,* realism has been a factor. Lord Willis originator of *The Blue Lamp* says of it:

'The Blue Lamp' was the first film to show the police with some degree of realism . . . It's difficult for people nowadays to understand exactly what was new because they have been so accustomed to police series, but it was literally the first film that took people behind the scenes in a police station. It was the first film, for example, which showed the parade of policemen that they used to have in those days before they went off on their beat taking instructions from their Superintendent. It was the first film that showed the kind of humdrum day-to-day life of a policeman behind the counter of a police station or on the beat and his relationships with his clients, as he called them in those days. (From interview for *Crime Writers* series).

The *Dixon* scripts Willis wrote were essentially folk tales, the production emanated from the Light Entertainment department of the BBC. They were laced with sentiment. That does not mean that the shows were without integrity. Quite the reverse, the warm and reassuring figure of Jack Warner would always appear at the end of a tale to tie up the end and point out the moral. He had an almost magical quality. But the time came in the early sixties when the image no longer seemed to reflect anything other than a kind of cosiness. There was a new urgency, new stirrings of social concern.

> *God is not nice*
> *He is not an uncle*
> *He is an earthquake*
> (old Hasidic text)

Jack Warner as Ted Willis'
everyday police constable,
(*above*) in the film *The Blue
Lamp* with Jimmy Hanley
and (*below*) in television's
Dixon of Dock Green

The Barlow phenomenon which blasted its way on to the small screen on 1962/63 erased Dixon as a figure of authority. Shortly after I created the character, it seemed to get out of control. In the early *Z Cars* scripts Barlow was portrayed as a dreamer, a man who would never escape from the confines of Newtown, a passed-over Detective Chief Inspector whose ideas of promotion were to be forever thwarted, and indeed his motivation for the establishment of the Crime Patrol was yet another vain attempt to add to his stature.

Although Alan Stratford Johns' portrayal of the Inspector must have had something to do with the subsequent development of Barlow's character, one can't help feeling that a lot of other subconscious forces were at work. The avidity with which the press greeted the concept of Barlow as the stern face of authority, the vengeful father, surprised me; I felt it was a stereotype which would have been automatically resisted in the production office. After all, it seemed an amazingly old-fashioned concept. But this love affair with authority, this identification with power, the decision to go with the stream rather than check it, seemed to me to have undercurrents which had nothing to do with making a police series, but which reflected a certain atavism in English life and in the English character which I had thought dead. If there are psychological roots for British fascism – they are here.

It is worth noting here that to a large extent the development of police series have been largely occasioned by what was

P.C. Jock Weir (Joseph Brady) and P.C. 'Fancy' Smith (Brian Blessed) as the crew of Z-Victor 1 in the first *Z Cars*

Stratford Johns as
Det. Chief Supt. Barlow

going on in other TV series rather than the outside world. *Z Cars* began as a reaction against Dixon.

I was lying, annoyingly ill, in 1961 monitoring police messages to pass the time and occasionally coming across incidents where it was obvious that the police were not coping. They seemed confused, lost and apparently young and inexperienced. The world that filtered through these fragmentary calls was so different from that of *Dixon* that I took the idea of a new series to Elwyn Jones, who was then head of a small but influential section of the BBC Drama Department.

The BBC was at that time expanding with the vigour of a Hoylesque universe, the trigger being the inception of BBC 2. They were in need of new material. Elwyn Jones sent me to Lancashire where he already had strong connections. The Lancashire police took me down to Kirby, an unfinished new-town outside of Liverpool with sharp social problems. A major shift in my ideas took place during my visits to Lancashire in the following three months. The strong Kirby background and particularly its social problems began to be reflected in the draft scripts.

It is ironic that, although I was determined to torpedo the *Dixon* series, I found myself following in the footsteps of Ted Willis who on researching *The Blue Lamp* discovered that police work was leading him directly into areas of social drama.

Apart from the fact that I'd never attempted to write any kind of working-class dialogue before, never mind Lancashire, the great difficulty I found was in trying to keep the story at street level. The temptation was to get back into the safety of the office, and to deal with it through Watt and Barlow. However, I think it was a strength of the series – and of the scripts – that we did keep it at the sharp end of police work, at that point where 'the lads' were constantly in collision with the public. I think the shape of the scripts, emphasising character and incident at the expense of the primacy of story, was probably correct at the time.

I say this because, after I left the series, I saw other writers succumb to the same temptation – to get off the streets and back into the office. In fact the subsequent history of *Z Cars* is that of the embourgoisement of everyone involved, the characters within the series, the actors, the writers, the producers – who knows, perhaps even the viewers. There was a slow distancing of it from the people it was concerned to portray.

Somewhere during this process Barlow and Watt lost their

accents and were promoted. *Softly Softly* was based on a new policing concept, the Regional Crime Squad, one of those crafty pluralistic ideas of the Home Office which allowed an overlap in the detection of crime. It was to become important when, to put it broadly, the Met went bent.

Whatever can be said of *Softly Softly* it was certainly not a radicalising series. Barlow's rise to high places corresponded with an increasingly right-wing approach to controversial matters such as drugs, squatters and Black power. Although to be fair his views in fact probably mirrored those of his opposite numbers in the real police force. Ted Willis (in the *Crime Writers* interview already quoted) puts this problem succinctly:

LORD WILLIS: *This is rather delicate ground, but I would think that the vast majority of police, the good majority of police, would support Enoch Powell's line on race. You never see that reflected in police series, because no-one wants to reflect it.*
INTERVIEWER: *Is the same true of corruption to some extent?*
LORD WILLIS: *I think it is. You destroy the myth if you run, week after week, a series in which you show absolutely corrupt coppers. You destroy not only the myth, but I would be opposed to it because I value the police very highly. I disagree with them on many things (as I've indicated) but I don't think we could survive in any society whether it's communist or fascist without a police force. I think we've probably got the least corrupt police force in the world, but that doesn't mean that there aren't quite a number of corrupt coppers.*

The major issue which separated *Softly Softly* from later police series was that of corruption. By the early seventies, tales of corruption in the Metropolitan CID had reached epidemic proportions. Frank Williamson, Cumbria's Chief Constable, had been called to investigate some of the aspects of this scandal. When, following his report, no action was taken, he resigned and later referred to the CID at Scotland Yard as a 'sea of villainy'. A concerted effort was made to keep the dimensions of this sea out of the newspapers, every case that came before the courts being declared subjudice. This, one would have thought, would have been the ideal opportunity for the police series.

The root principle which is applied to police corruption is that of the rotten apple. It is the conventional wisdom of the day that one apple in the barrel has the capability of corrupting the rest. The extension of this axiom, by definition, is that the others are not corrupt to begin with and the rogue apple is in some way a deviant.

Ted Willis

Stratford Johns as Barlow
in *Softly, Softly*

Derek Martin as Detective
Inspector Fred Pyall and Billy
Cornelius as Detective
Sergeant Eric Lethridge in
a series of plays on BBC
television *Law and Order*

G. F. Newman, who wrote *Law and Order,* the series of plays produced by Tony Garnett and screened on BBC in spring 1978, took another view: the apples in the CID barrel were continually going rotten and that if they weren't in this permanent state of fermentation, they would not be able to do their job, which is to protect us from criminal despotism.

'I wanted to show the police,' Newman has said, 'as they've never been shown before on the television screen, or any other screen come to that, and part of the intention was to actually make a film about the police that stated the case as it is in present day. So anyone who then came along wanting to make a police film or a police series would actually have to take this film out and see how the police work. Whether we've achieved that I don't know but it was part of the intention.'

What Newman wants the public to recognise is that we are asking the police to combat crime with the aid of rules which are patently unworkable. And since deep down we all know this, what Newman is getting at is not the dishonesty of the police force but the hypocrisy of our society. And one of the main targets that he and Garnett were gunning for was the police series.

'I think the main problem,' Newman adds, 'is that the people who make the series, the people who write them, the people who direct them just don't know the realities of police, villain and judiciary. They just don't know policemen and criminals. They haven't experienced policing a metropolis, they haven't experienced crime, so they have nothing to relate to. All they can relate to in fact are things they've seen on television. If you accept that television is art – I mean it's bread and butter art I suppose – then art should imitate life. But all television is doing is imitating other art, I mean they're just imitating Kojak and things like that, American television police fiction.'

Softly Softly's answer to 'sea of villainy' was a single episode concerning a Constable who accepts as a gift a fountain pen from a local publican/villain. When the man is finally arrested Barlow, if my memory is correct, goes into a furious denunciation of corruption based on the rotten apples principle. In fact I believe he used the phrase. At that time some hundred policemen were under investigation at New Scotland Yard.

The problem with the rotten apple theory is that it not only continues to uphold what Lord Willis calls the Myth but it also upholds what I would call the Lie. The Myth is that the British police are incorruptible, that they don't perjure themselves etc., that they don't manipulate evidence etc. and that if they do they are probably off their heads.

The Lie is an attitude in the media that anything approaching reality on television undermines the whole basis of law in this country, that the audience is not mature enough to face the contradictions involved, and that they must be protected. It was this fiction which the *Law and Order* plays sought to puncture. It was not the integrity of the police force that was at stake but the credibility of the television services.

The protection of the public from reality is quite a different aim from that of providing the public with good entertainment. Although the two are not mutually exclusive, neither are they self-cancelling.

While Gordon Newman and Tony Garnett were beginning work on the first of the *Law and Order* scripts, *The Sweeney* made by Euston Films hit the network. It was pure escapist entertainment – 1970's style.

Euston Films was a spin-off of Thames Television and had been formed a few years earlier with the idea of producing drama series films. Apart from its initial cost, film has advantages in overseas sales but the prime aim here was to circumvent the heavy overheads of TV studios. There was also a case to be made out for the creative advantages of film, but this was never a major concern of the television industry.

Euston Films began with a series called *Special Branch*. It is difficult to imagine, with a war on in Ulster and the streets of London echoing to the sound of broken glass from Irish bombers, that anyone would develop a series which made not the slightest reference to the Branch's primary purpose of existence (it was created in order to combat the Fenian movement) nor to the contemporary political situation. Nevertheless Euston Films managed to do so. Patrick Mower ran through the series, gun in hand finding strings of missing pearls in the more exotic parts of Kensington and dabbling in African power politics. It was if you like a throw-back to the old Wolsey pictures with Mower's depiction of the policeman – despite a contemporary toughness – essentially middle-class. The only interesting feature about *Special Branch* was that it produced many of the people who were subsequently to be deployed in *The Sweeney*. These included the director, Tom Clegg and the producer Ted Childs.

The Sweeney was about the Flying Squad. It was a notion of my brother, Ian Kennedy Martin, who took it to Euston in the form of a ninety minute pilot. To paraphrase G. F. Newman's Inspector Pyle, *Softly Softly* was 'well overdue', and Ian couldn't help reflecting that its continuance on the screen owed less to its popularity than to a loss of nerve at the BBC. That is that if they took it off, they would have to replace it with something with a contemporary edge. And the con-

John Thaw as Detective Inspector Regan with Dennis Waterman as his Sergeant in the television series *The Sweeney*

troversy over the original *Z Cars* was still somehow lodged in its collective subconscious.

However, Euston had no such qualms. They took it on the assumption they were making an extension of *Special Branch*. Ian had other ideas. He requested that I should be taken on as part of the package and insisted that John Thaw should play Regan. The whole thing was to be built round Thaw.

I was in two minds about the project. It had been fifteen years since I had written for a police series – *Z Cars* – except for a small stint with *Redcap* – again a John Thaw vehicle. I was also divorced and broke.

In the previous year I had co-written with Gordon Newman a film for Tony Garnett. This was to be the quintessential police film. It never got off the ground, but from Gordon Newman I had picked up a great deal of information about Metropolitan CID – their language and style. This was to be of immense use in *The Sweeney*.

I was also worried about the degree of corruption which appeared to exist in the Yard. And it was obvious that *The Sweeney* was not going to prove the vehicle to reflect this, what with its very commercial management and its glossy colour. In fact Euston had a style of lighting which made it difficult to make a slum look unattractive. So the question which faced one was not so much of exposing the truth but of not maintaining the Lie.

This may seem nit-picking to someone not engaged in series drama, but this was a period of what might be called negative networking, where despite the appearance of a commitment on the part of the television companies to take risks, in fact the opposite was the case. The policy of retrenchment was extremely difficult to penetrate but the freshness of the company, its lack of association with any of the dullards of the TV Drama scene, the fact that there is a television law in which freedom is in inverse proportion to the amount of money used, and that Thames were spending the barest minimum on the series, made me think that something could be done with the scripts.

No sooner were the contracts signed than Ian resigned from the series on the grounds that his original intention would not be carried out. (There was no night shooting for instance and the Flying Squad work almost exclusively at night.) I soldiered on, and I'm glad I did so. I think the scripts that I wrote, were better than the ones for *Z Cars* – and contributed to the success of the series.

What *The Sweeney* became was simply an action adventure series based on the Flying Squad with the accent on anarchy and humour. It gained its sense of reality from the remarkable performances of Thaw and Waterman, two most unselfish actors, whose influence on the series extended well beyond the set.

The Sweeney has been described as being American influenced, an imitation of the West Coast shows. Its success has also been credited to its violence, a catch-all which in the beginning was even used as the promotional material.

Neither of these points is wholly true. *The Sweeney* was an uneven programme, but at its best there was nothing that the West Coast could produce to match its originality and performance, if anything the traffic in ideas flowed the other way. As for the violence, this was the first time a British audience had been confronted by a British television series made on film rather than videotape. If enthusiastic sound editors were a little indiscriminate and slapped screaming tyres on every car shot, and if the editors cut the action sequences for maximum effect, then this was what video-bound series such as *Z Cars* would have loved to have done – given the same facilities.

From the point of view of the writer, series format allowed a kind of anarchy to develop which I have not seen before in a television series – it was a world of vanity and self-mockery. If the enemy at the door was the Governor, the rubber-heels of A 10 (the branch that investigates detectives) were always just round the corner. Regan was always being crossed by other departments, being spurned by ladies – and always under threat of suspension. He is a man continually on the balls of his feet, escaping from week to week – often from the consequences of his own folly.

The world of *The Sweeney* was a world where the statement of a self-confessed murderer develops into a wrangle over newspaper rights; where a young officer deputed to watch a lonely farmhouse, gets forgotten and becomes ill with exposure; where helicopters buzz out of the sky with loudspeakers booming at Regan to 'piss off'. Through this jungle Regan pursues his fetish of the girl with the German steel helmet and longs for the days when England hacked its way to victory in the World Cup. 'Where are you now Nobby, when we need you?'

The imitators that sprang up, following the success of the series were *Target* and *The Professionals*. They certainly took the violence from *The Sweeney* under the erroneous belief that that was what made *The Sweeney* popular.

To the extent that *The Sweeney* spawned these imitators, it is good that it has ended. But as long as the Police Series remains not so much a *genre* but the prevailing iconography of television drama, there will be others.

There is no reason why these should not be of good quality. But this will require a more courageous approach from programme makers.

Further Reading

Ian Kennedy Martin: *The Sweeney* (Futura, 1975)

G. F. Newman: *Sir, You Bastard* (New English Lib., 1975)

John Hopkins: *This Story of Yours* (Modern Playwrights, 9. Penguin Books, 1969); *Find Your Way Home* (Penguin Books, 1971; French 1975)

Michael Marland ed.: *Z Cars: four television scripts* (Longman, 1968)

Elwyn Jones: *Softly Softly: four scripts* (Longman, 1976)

Ted Willis: *Hunter's Walk* (Severn House, 1976)

The authenticity of Police Series

Another view of the development of the police series on television was given by Elwyn Jones, creator of *Softly Softly* in a *Crime Writers* interview.

INTERVIEWER: *'Softly Softly' provided a great deal of information about the developing role of the police in the late sixties and early seventies. Why didn't you deal more with the major issue in the police forces at the time, that of corruption?*

ELWYN JONES: *Well, I don't think in fact that corruption was the major thing in the police force in the United Kingdom, except the Met. I think this was far more a Metropolitan problem – because, as one Met. man said a great many years ago, 'we have cosmopolitan problems' – which in fact you don't encounter even in cities as big and as involved as Liverpool and Manchester. I mean, there are bad cops, but the scale of corruption outside the Met. is simply not so great. And I don't think it was therefore an important issue.*

INTERVIEWER: *Is the weekly police series ever going to be able to give us an authentic picture of what it's like to be a policeman?*

ELWYN JONES: *It's a question of what you mean by authentic – you can get fairly near the truth, but all drama is compression and therefore you can't dramatise, or you can't dramatise interestingly, for a long period the inevitable troughs of boredom that occur in any job. If someone is out on the beat, or sitting in a car and he's bored out of his mind, you can suggest that, but you can't go on stating it because it isn't interesting. So out of compression you get a kind of distortion. The other thing on the same sort of level is that there are some things too horrific for you even to show – certainly to a family audience at any time of day or night, and therefore you are softening. 'Major Incident' (in the 'Softly Softly' series) was described as harrowing, but you know, it was as near the truth as I felt we could go, but it certainly wasn't anything like the whole truth.*

Police stories – and after

The television policeman has become a popular hero on both sides of the Atlantic. *Kojak* and *Starsky and Hutch* are as familiar to British viewers as any British police series. This success has been viewed with some unease by the more thoughtful writers. Ed McBain had this to say in his book *Blood Relatives*: 'Carella always turned off the television set whenever a cop show came on. He sometimes wondered if doctors turned off the set when a doctor show came on. Or lawyers. Or forest rangers. Or private eyes. Carella didn't know any private eyes. He knew a lot of cops, though, and hardly any of them behaved the way television cops did. But a lot of them watched television cop shows. Probably gave them ideas on how to deal with the good guys and the bad guys . . . Television cops were dangerous. They made real life cops feel like heroes instead of hard working slobs.'

John Hopkins, the writer who contributed more scripts to *Z Cars* than anyone else, wrote a stage play *This Story Of Yours* (later filmed as *The Offence*) which is a study of the effects of a lifetime of policework on a man with his own personal problems. Hopkins' play was an attempt to see the police as individual human beings, not a homogeneous group to praise or condemn according to social or political attitudes. This view is presented with great conviction in the books of Joseph Wambaugh, a Los Angeles police sergeant who turned to writing after graduating in English Literature at night school. His books show police work from the point of view of the low ranking policemen

David Soul as Hutch and Michael Glaser as Starsky
in the American television series *Starsky and Hutch*

who actually deal with the job at street level. As
in the Hopkins' play a great deal of emphasis is
given to the emotional strain of being in con-
tinual contact with human debris and misery
and its potentially brutalising effect.

Another police officer turned writer is the
American Dorothy Uhnak, and in her book
Policewoman she states her view of the situation
very clearly 'If I have acquired a certain sceptic-

ism and a certain hardness, it was a necessary
growing process, for a police officer cannot be a
sponge absorbing the misery and degradation he
encounters. But on the other hand, he cannot let
the hardness penetrate to the centre of him, or he
will cease to be a human being.

'If through the years I have been shocked or
disillusioned or sickened by the people I have
encountered, or the situations in which I have

Three American police
series heroes. (*Above*)
Telly Savalas as Kojak;
(*right*) Karl Malden, with
Michael Douglas, in
*The Streets of San
Francisco*; and (*below*)
Peter Falk as Columbo

become involved, I do not now regret my career, for I feel my life in police work has been a tremendously important education.'

The Swedish husband and wife team, Maj Sjowall and Per Wahloo, wrote many successful police stories together. *The Locked Room, The Man on the Balcony, The Laughing Policeman* are all good books with a very individual feeling. Inspector Martin Beck is the decent and honest, if rather lugubrious, policeman in charge of the investigations. As the cases proceed Beck finds himself questioning the nature of his job, of crime and justice, and of society itself. Wahloo also wrote *Murder on the Thirty-First Floor* and *The Steel Spring,* books which have been compared to Orwell and Kafka. In them he uses the format of the police story to look at the ways in which society is in danger of developing.

The different treatments of the police in crime fiction are part of the questioning of moral and social attitudes that has become characteristic of society today. This presents some problems for the writers, as Brian Garfield said in an interview for the *Crime Writers* television series. 'I think it means that the crime writers have to be faster on their feet. It's probably a matter of simply keeping up with the changes that are taking place in public attitudes. I think we've had an infusion of cynicism in the last decade or two, which not only made it possible for there to be a Watergate, but also made it possible for us not to be surprised for there to be a Watergate. I think the fact that everyone takes corruption in human society for granted makes it a bit more difficult for the writer to deal in clear moral terms.'

7
New patents pending
by H.R.F. Keating

What of the future? What will writers tackling the subject of crime give us tomorrow? Are any new patents pending? The answer to those questions is twofold.

The first part depends to a large extent on what sort of a world, what sort of crimes, will face writers in the coming years. And to predict the course of our crazy planet for even the next decade is to risk being proved ridiculously wrong perhaps even before the words I type this morning have reached the bookshops. But to some extent one can also extrapolate from current trends, say what tomorrow will bring from looking at today. Yet it is by no means easy to see clearly when one does that. I calculate that the batches of books I review for *The Times* work out at a weekly average of three volumes considered, close on 150 a year, and that for every book I contrive a mention for there are perhaps two others that have to sink traceless. So many facts. Not a few of them contradictory. Drawing conclusions then is rather more chancy than looking at horses' names in a newspaper and trying from all those 1s, 2s and 0s in front of them, together with a few incalculables like jockeys' temperaments, the effect of raindrops on grass-covered earth and the wiles of trainers, to pick the winner of the Grand National a month before it's run.

But there is a second answer to our questions, though it is an answer which perhaps depends more on feel than fact. It is to try to see the whole course of the art of crime writing up till now and from that to say where it is likely to go. It is prognosticating by internal logic rather than external.

Let us look first at the answers derivable from external factors. As Frederic Dannay (Ellery Queen) said in one of the interviews made for the *Crime Writers* television series, 'a trend doesn't really start with the writer, a trend starts with the world'. And in the world new discoveries and new fashions daily make a difference to the writer's material. I have yet to read a murder story where it's done by laser, but I'm certain it won't be long before I do. And I'm sure, too, that the fashions we have recently seen in disaster books following on from Richard Martin Stern's *Towering Inferno,* in 'Is Hitler alive, or is it his sperm-transplanted son?' books, or in 'How they stole the fissile material' books, will be followed soon because of the spate of political kidnappings in Europe and elsewhere by book after book with kidnappings of that sort as their plot spring.

In Britain we had only to have a newspaper outcry about anomalies in rape sentencing to get in due course at least two books about rape, Jacqueline Wilson's *Making Hate* and *The Rapist* by Michael Kenyon, both excellent treatments of the theme, rising above the day-to-day sensationalisms to look at it whole and steadily. In America the CIA had only to hit a sticky patch for, it sometimes seemed, half the villains in half the suspense stories to be CIA backed. Guessing ahead on these lines, I would expect, for instance, that Eric Ambler's study of 'the able criminal', as the criminologists call the really big boys who almost always get away with it, *Send No More Roses,* will not the the last in that particular field. But beyond that I refuse to chance my arm.

Yet some major movements in the global outlook we can safely see as continuing at least for some time to come, though even here prophecy seems often designed merely to show up the prophet, as witness Orwell's *1984* now within measurable distance as a date but not really very accurate as a picture of our world. Still, I will venture on the platitude that today we see more violence all about us than once we did and that in the immediate tomorrow this will probably get worse. So that strain of violence that has been present in sensation literature from the year dot, though it had a period of absence from the detective story proper, will presumably be even more noticeable in the crime books we are soon to get.

And that will be no bad thing. Unthinking people deplore violence on the printed page as if it was the violence they fear in real life. But, of course, it is not. It isn't violence: it's only black squiggles on white paper. But the squiggles make us, if they're good squiggles, undergo the experience of violence. They enable us, therefore, to see violence in its proper perspective. To realise, for instance, that without a degree of

Jacqueline Wilson

violence the world could not go on. 'A child is not born without blood,' as the Indian proverb has it. The good man must at some point knock down the bad man. The foot must squash the poisonous insect. Thanks to the crime novel with violence in it, we can bear to look at the violence all about us. And the violent within us.

If it is safe to predict growing violence in at least the world that the crime novel deals with, then it is safe too to hazard that the more and more intense interest in the sexual in that same world will also go on growing. And that crime books of all sorts will more and more reflect that. Already the situation is very different from what it was barely twenty years ago. Read a quite ordinary whodunnit today and, likely as not, the detective, a sober policeman, will not get to hear about his case until he has woken up in the morning in the conjugal bed (or sometimes not) and reflected for a little on how well the sexual shenanigans went the night before.

For myself, I could wish that we could manage without that sort of publisher-stipulated sex in the crime novel. Much more often than not it adds nothing truly relevant to the business in hand, beyond at the crudest level inducing most readers to turn a page. But I will by no means predict that some splendid self-denying ordinance will obliterate this trend within the next ten years. I suspect even that it has yet to reach its maximum level.

Some sexual description, even on occasion the most basic, does, however, add directly to what a crime novel can say. It is easy to see, for example, how a man's character can be illuminated by plain unvarnished description of the way he goes about making love. Is he thoughtful? Is he weak? Has he a strain of violence in him? From the answers there we can get an answer to the question 'Is he the sort of person who would commit one kind of murder but not another?'

We have had already novels of this sort, really making use of the sexual to tell a crime story, though fewer than might be expected of a society to which the adjective 'permissive' has been chain-locked. But sex is a fiendishly difficult subject to tackle, as the large number of 'publisher's orders' writers who come a cropper over it testifies.

It has occurred to me, however, as a person who grew up in the pre-permissive days, that this difficulty may be one that is more to be found among older writers than younger. Take for example a novelist like Jacqueline Wilson, whose fine treatment of a rape theme I have already mentioned. She was born only in 1945 and was thus just sixteen in 1961, the year of the *Lady Chatterley* obscenity trial which is perhaps the most

Reginald Hill

convenient date for the start of the Permissive Society. She seems able to write of sexual intimacies in a way that is neither prurient nor jokey, something which writers a great deal more experienced often fail to achieve.

Of much the same vintage is Reginald Hill. Take his 1978 book *A Pinch of Snuff* which deals with that most awkward of subjects, violence in sex. (The 'snuff' of his title refers to the so-called 'snuff movies', pornographic films in which sexual thrills are provided by the actual killing of the star: when a writer of an older generation, Michael Underwood, used the same title only four years earlier it was for a story centring on the theft of snuff boxes). The crime here is murder, but it is a murder chosen because it was committed against a background of sexual violence, a club devoted to showing blue movies, possibly even of the 'snuff' variety. The victim, too, is a former private school headmaster about whom there are rumours of unpleasant sexually motivated violence and who is also found dead with the marks of a thrashing on his body. The whole, then, is simultaneously a study of a problem that exercises a great fascination on today's society and a whodunnit that grips readers by the simple device of their wanting to solve the mystery.

Certainly we could do with many more examples of this sort of book, and I record a personal hope that it becomes a leading trait in the crime writing of the immediate future. Perhaps as more and more writers born into the post-war world take a greater share of the market this fond wish will come true.

Yet not all the writers who can deal with sex are mere striplings. A splendid instance of the opposite lies in Stanley Ellin's novel, *Mirror, Mirror,* published in America in 1972, in Britain a year later, and winner in France in the following year of the Grand Prix du Meilleur Roman Policier Etranger, but written somewhat earlier and rejected by publishers then as being too explicit. It is a book that depends solely on sexual fantasy for the solution of its central mystery, a solution that involves unravelling the key character's sexual life right back to mother's kisses and right on to a time-of-writing fetish over Swedish underwear. Till now it has had, in my experience, no true successor. But if ours really is the age of a beneficial sexual explicitness it ought to have successors if not by the hundred (the feat is difficult) then at least by the score.

The Permissive Society is, almost by definition, a society that encourages moral ambiguity. Where it is all right to do almost anything (if that is not describing the Permissive Society in terms altogether too blunt) then there are almost no rules. This is both a severe handicap for the crime novel and a

challenge to it. It is a handicap, for instance, in that the traditional detective novel depended basically on there being rules of behaviour. These the murderer himself flouted in the most extreme form (though it would be well to ponder the quite considerable number of traditional detective stories where in fact the murderer was not an out-and-out villain and was, if not let go scot free, allowed at least to take the gentlemanly way out or to be killed in a convenient *deus ex machina* accident). But the existence of accepted rules also gave detective-story authors the chance to make full use of deviations from them as the essential clues. Was a character late for tea? Then almost certainly they had been up to no good, either misguidedly muddying the trail or otherwise providing some sort of red herring.

Julian Symons

But an age where nothing, or very little, is fixed or sacred is also, as I have said, a challenge to the writer of crime stories. A challenge to describe that age, to use that moral ambiguity. And that challenge has been magnificently taken up by some of the authors of the past two decades. Notably, of course, by Patricia Highsmith, whose contribution to the art is discussed elsewhere in this book. But there have been others who have, not indeed followed in her footsteps, but gone along parallel paths. The most considerable of these to my mind is Julian Symons, one of those blessed crime writers (Stanley Ellin is another) who do not give us the same sort of book time and again but range almost the whole field in a succession of surprises. Every now and again, especially in the course of his later career, Julian Symons has tackled a subject reflecting

the marvellous good/bad moral ambiguity of our times, as for instance in *The Colour of Murder* where the chief suspect can remember nothing of the events leading to his trial or in the highly unflattering study of police work (once it was axiomatic that the police, though they might bungle, were never bad) of *The Progress of a Crime*. Or look at these words spoken by the hero in *The End of Solomon Grundy* (They are nearly the last in the book):

'Which of us is innocent?' he said gently, almost chidingly. 'And you said just now that I was not responsible. Do you mean that there is no such thing as responsibility?'

Then the revolver went off.

This exploitation of our moral uncertainties is, again, a trend I would expect to see running ahead for a good many years to come. It can be detected in the work of other old stagers (not to say old masters) such as Joan Fleming and Evelyn Berckman and it is, of course, a mainstay of the Argentinian writer Borges, though despite his frequent use of the detective-story form I think there is little point in considering him as a crime writer.

But the using of moral ambiguity to produce intriguing crime literature is not confined to exceptionally practised artists. It can be found too in the work of writers who have so far published comparatively little, and are therefore perhaps yet better marker birds. I refer for example to the books of Desmond Cory, such as *Bennett* in which he exploits every trick of illusion, down to a fake list of 'other books by' in advance of his title-page, to make the reader think about the supposedly secure bases of his world, or to those of David Fletcher, again a young author of whom it is reasonable to expect a good deal in the years to come. But standing somewhat above these by virtue of his remarkable success in a short time is the American Gregory Mcdonald, author so far of only four books yet winner of Mystery Writer of America awards for the best first novel and the best paperback of its year. His teasing, keep-up-if-you-can accounts of crime in Boston, often with a hero who is more than three parts crook, well illustrate what can be done in accepting this particular challenge of our times.

I would not like to say that our uncertainties are directly responsible for a general rise in the crime rate, both in Europe and America. A crime rate, for one thing, is by no means an easy thing to ascertain. Crimes fail to get reported. At different periods different actions are considered more or less criminal. Statistics are often a matter of interpretation. But certainly it is frequently claimed not simply that there is more crime today (and thus more for the writer concerned with crime to write about, more and different) but that its impact is more widely spread. The most humdrum of housewives, the most ordinary of citizens, can become victim these days of decidedly bizarre crimes.

So another trend it is reasonable to suppose will continue in the world of crime fiction is for stories based on the sickening excitements that can befall, not your James Bonds or your Sir John Applebys, but Mr Smith and more particularly Mrs Smith. Again I cite as an example the novels of Jacqueline Wilson, whose heroines and villains are almost always suburban through and through. And to her I might add some of the books of Margaret Yorke where the people to whom things happen are likely to be the ordinary village dwellers of today's England (a different type altogether from the semi-mythical

Margaret Yorke

Brian Garfield

village dwellers of legendary Mayhem Parva in the Golden Age of the detective puzzle). There are other authors I might have chosen here, but the trend is clear.

A rising crime rate, the whittling away of once firm moral rules, an increasing manifestation of the sexual, all these are almost bound to produce strong reactions. And it is a fairly safe bet that we have not seen the last of such movements in our society. So, once again, one can expect the crime story, that almost instant mirror of contemporary mores, to reflect this trend. We have already had the novels of Brian Garfield in America showing what might happen in various vigilante situations, a theme used in Britain at least once, too, by the prolific and excellent John Wainwright. I might also quote just a phrase from *The Loo Sanction* by 'Trevanian', a spy send-up set in London, in which the city's much-prized swinging chicks are scathingly described as 'anti-war, socially committed, sexually liberated, dull, dull, dull'.

John Wainwright

Indeed, even as long ago as the end of the Swinging Sixties there were signs of the reaction to the Right to be observed in the current batches of crime stories, much the same sort of pendulum swing, though in the opposite direction, that occurred in the espionage novel when Eric Ambler in the days just before the 1939 War introduced the hero who was a progressive in politics. I have in mind the novels of William Haggard (rather more leaning to espionage than crime, and so perhaps not quite proper for this particular study, though significant for their popularity) with their strongly expressed scorn for 'softy fools' and the police novels that John Wainwright was producing at that time with their confident dismissals of 'airy-fairy do-gooders' and their belief that the law had to be bent a little to be a properly effective instrument.

Another manifestation of disquiet over a morally ambiguous society is the cult of nostalgia, and this too has been reflected in crime stories and is likely (unless the world suddenly gets to seem a much safer place) to go on for a good many years yet. Thus we have had in the past few years a rash of crime stories set in Victorian days. I have even been responsible for one myself, *A Remarkable Case of Burglary*. The particular period, the Victorian, that has become especially popular, in for instance the now quite long series of novels by Peter Lovesey or in the best-selling *Laura* by Jean Stubbs, is significant. That was a time we now see, rightly or wrongly, as being especially stable, an era in which you could expect the same thing tomorrow as today only a bit better, a society in which people knew their places but where some upward movement was always allowed for provided it sprang from a proper energy and determination. Again I could list other names in support, but I will content myself with pointing out that different historical times have also abruptly seemed possible to the crime writer with mystery stories like Jeremy

Peter Lovesey

Potter's *Death in the Forest* (1083 and all that) and Ellis Peters' *A Morbid Taste for Bones* (medieval Wales). Perhaps these are precursors of a considerable upsurge in historical whodunnits of all periods.

Allied to the nostalgia novel set in a period clearly removed from our own troubled day there is the crime book that harks back to a past still linked to our present discontents. This, what might be called the story with roots, seems to be coming more and more into favour with authors and presumably readers too.

I take as a prime example many if not all of the much-praised novels of Anthony Price. Anthony Price is a writer who happens to have strong historical interests, mostly in the area of military history. Ingeniously he has contrived to combine this love with his equal love for the espionage novel, the story of plot and counter-plot. So that typically he takes some facet of

Anthony Price

military history – it might be the Battle of the Somme – that especially grips his imagination and so gives him that strong purpose essential to good writing, and he devises a plot in today's world that for some reason depends on knowledge of that now distant battle. The device has the effect of giving his books a considerable depth, a rooting in real life. And it is this, I imagine, that to a great extent accounts for their success with their readers.

But again the motivation is clear: the books become assertions in a world of flux that there is some stability, that we are not without roots. There have been other writers who have used variations of this method with success as well. I name only John Gardner, prolific in other branches of the genre, with his 1978 book *The Dancing Dodo* where the mystery to be solved is linked with the heroic days of the air war against Hitler, and Michael Sinclair with *The Masterplayers,* also 1978, which delves back into obscure, but romantic, Romanian nineteenth-century history. Both I see as being in some sort of vanguard.

Again in a world where moral values are no longer axiomatic there would appear to be more point in using the novel, even the crime novel, even the most frivolous-seeming crime novel, in order to assert a personal belief in whatever values particularly appeal to the writer. So the crime novel that preaches or teaches or pleads is to be more and more expected.

A good many of those that we have already seen of this sort have been set in a future some years distant from their time of writing. And there they generally prognosticate a bad time, by way of warning us of our present inadequacies. I have in mind such books as Ted Willis's *The Churchill Commando* with its imaginary picture of a Right-inclined militarist take-over bid, or the portrait of a Britain wire-tapped and wriggling that was given us by Paul Ferris in *The Detective* or of a Britain where no man keeps faith in *A Patriot for Hire* by Andrew Sinclair. And there have been others, enough to constitute a trend or at least a trendlet.

A slightly different attitude to teaching society where it needs teaching can be seen in such books as John Wainwright's *The Peppercorn Kill,* a decidedly strong indictment of the cruelties inherent in our prisons today, or in Mary Higgins Clark's warning to America on capital punishment, *A Stranger Is Watching*. Dickens in his day did not hesitate to use the popular novel as a direct instrument of social reform, and I myself would not be sorry to see the crime story being used in this way in the years to come.

But I must confess I would be less happy to see another

Mary Higgins Clark

Paul Erdman

similar trend flourishing, though I suspect strongly that it will do so. This is the sort of book that has been called faction as opposed to fiction, the book which derives its strength from a close adherence to a set of known facts generally in some political context and often, but not always, used to tick us off for present short-comings. I suppose the best-known example of the sub-genre as a whole is Frederick Forsyth's *The Day of the Jackal*. But many others seek to use their facts as a base on which to build a theory, about who killed President Kennedy or Martin Luther King or about some other similar event. To my mind in all such books the facts almost always get in the way of the story, and a crime novel ought to tell a story and, being in the last analysis fiction, ought to work with the tools of fiction. But I cannot see the trend for faction coming to an early end. It seems to appeal to some facet in the make-up of the seventies reader.

Another new development, with something often of the warning about it, is what one might dub the 'whopaysit', the crime novel with a financial background, generally of a fairly massive sort. The prime instance of a writer of this kind, I suppose, and one remarkable if only because of his quantative success, is Paul Erdman, author of *The Billion Dollar Killing*,

Janwillem van de Wetering

Dorothy Uhnak

The Silver Bears and *The Crash of '79*. To these might be added a series of books with an industrial spy or counterspy as hero written by Ken Follett, of which *The Bear Raid* is a good example, and a book by Peter Tanous and Paul Rubinstein, *The Petrodollar Takeover*. Often, alas, in this sort of thing financial knowhow seems to predominate over storytelling skill, but we might in the immediate future hope for better luck in a potentially fascinating field.

Far removed from figures-juggling but another symptom of our unstable world is the cult of mysticism. At a time when orthodox religion appears to be less and less attractive to the common man it is to be expected that the less orthodox, ranging from Zen Buddhism to witchcraft, comes to the fore. And, trailing not very far behind, come the crime books with various sorts of mystic experiences as parts of their plots, or in the case of Ira Levin's *Rosemary's Baby* as the plot centre. How different from the days when the detective story was nothing if not strictly rational.

The symptom manifests itself often less in the whole concept of a book than in its incidentals, but one writer of some esteem who consistently puts the irrational in a central place in his crime novels is the Dutchman, and former Zen disciple, Janwillem van de Wetering. Watch out for more along these lines. And more mingling, too, of the dear old ghost story and crime, as in Kenneth O'Hara's 1978 book, *The Ghost of Thomas Penry* and John Gardner's *The Werewolf Trace* (Hitler lives plus parapsychology) and Elleston Trevor's *The Theta Syndrome* (Hospital murder with ESP overtones).

I suppose that one of the major upheavals in the Western hemisphere in our time has been the strides forward made by women in what was once largely a man's stable world. So where is the crime novel with the woman hero? Answer: It sprang to life with Miss Marple? Hardly. Feminine though she was, and successful as she was as a sleuth, she solved her cases largely by taking advantage of what were looked on as the more negative aspects of life, quietness and intuition. But there have been some new women crime heroes, Dorothy Uhnak's Christie Opara or P. D. James' Cordelia Gray, though none, I think, taking a really dominating position. Yet I cannot but believe that the day will come. And soon.

Let me conclude this necessarily piecemeal survey of our poor old world today and the way crime writing is likely to reflect it by considering a theory I owe to the popular philosopher (and occasional crime novelist) Colin Wilson, author of *The Outsider*. He has asked what sort of murder it is that particularly attracts the average man from generation to generation. Once it was, as Orwell pointed out in a celebrated essay *Decline of the English Murder,* the killing for the sake of respectability. Orwell's formula for what then to your *News of the World* reader was the perfect murder was a killer who was a little man of the professional class living in some neat suburb in a semi-detached (suspicious sounds through thin walls) holding office in the local Conservative party or Nonconformist church who nourished a guilty passion for his secretary and eventually murdered with much careful planning (and one fatal flaw). Then, in the post-war years, when respectability began to count for less, it was the sex murder. Now, when perhaps, just perhaps, we have got sex where we can see it straight, it begins to be the murder for the sake of publicity that seems most glamorous, the murder to become an image in a world where images are deliberately created daily by the dozen. If the theory is right – and it's anyhow attractive – then a book like *The Season of the Machete* by the American James Patterson, in which a mass-murderer's motive is precisely publicity for himself, is going to be the first of a considerable stream. We shall see.

So much for what the world imposes, or may impose, on our sort of fiction: laser murder and other new gadgetries, kidnap stories, stories featuring the new master criminals probably with a strong financial angle, exploitation of the moral ambiguity of our times with various reactions to that, into backlash rigour, into escapist mysticism, into nostalgia and the safe past, into admonitions to us to mend our collective ways, together with more sex, and simultaneously perhaps books where a woman takes a clearly leading role, and more violence especially seen as affecting more ordinary people.

Remember, however, that at the same time that all or any of these new developments are flourishing almost all the old sub-species will continue their merry ways, if the past is anything to go by. The classic detective story in the Golden Age pattern still flourishes, after all, in the hands of writers like Elizabeth Lemarchand and Catherine Aird or in America Emma Lathen and Harry Kemelman, not to mention those splendid figures from the past still with us and writing, people like Gladys Mitchell, Josephine Bell, Edmund Crispin, Michael Innes, Christianna Brand and Elizabeth Ferrars. Long may they entertain us in their traditional way.

And on the other side of the Atlantic the classic private-eye story not only leads the way with Ross Macdonald but pushes out new shoots with Robert B. Parker and his Boston shamus Spenser, with the Jewish gumshoes operating in Hollywood of Andrew Bergman and Roger L. Simon, with, to my mind the

Joseph Hansen

Joseph Wambaugh

best of them all, Joseph Hansen's Dave Brandstetter, homosexual and singleminded in pursuit of the hidden truth. Even on this side of the Atlantic the private-eye has risen to effective life, notably in the adventures of that put-upon Cockney, Hazell, as told by P. B. Yuill. While both in England and America the more recent but absolutely well-established sub-genre of the police procedural goes from strength to strength in the hands of British writers like John Wainwright, Laurence Henderson and John Rossiter and American authors old and new like Ed McBain, Dell Shannon and Joseph Wambaugh.

The adventure story proliferates in the hands of a score of fine writers from Desmond Bagley to Duncan Kyle, from Hammond Innes to Alastair McLean, all writing hard now and likely to write for many years ahead in their chosen styles. While the Gothic novel (in its modern meaning), the story of a girl caught up in some grim wickedness, for a time kept rather under a cloud, has recently risen sharply in public honour with an increasing number of successful practitioners in America (where the sub-genre flourishes in the form, more esteemed there than here, of original paperbacks) and in Britain with such writers as Gwendoline Butler and Jean Stubbs.

But what of the changes in the *genre* that seem to be occurring from within as opposed to those dictated from without, the future that can be discerned perhaps from looking at the literary past?

It seems to me that one major movement can be detected. It is that the crime story is steering itself back into the general current of fiction. It has been slowly doing so for a long time, and I think the process is accelerating. Two of the speakers at the recent Second International Congress of Crime Writers in New York confirmed my long-held view. Brian Garfield, not only a writer of very successful suspense stories but also a student of the *genre,* declared firmly that 'the mystery is no longer a category' while Joan Kahn, doyenne of American mystery editors, was equally certain that the genre was 'moving towards the mainstream'.

I'm not sure but that Sherlock Holmes wasn't to blame for it ever having taken on a separate existence of its own. Doyle's stories were so immensely successful, Holmes took on such an independent being with those letters coming into 221B Baker Street, those mourning armbands after the Reichenbach business, that fashion for deerstalkers, those plays and those films, that a special separate sort of factory for making imitations and contraries seemed to spring up in his wake spawning the classic detective story which flourished so well, lived so long and is, as I have said, by no means dead yet. But it is perhaps lying down. And while it is quiescent other crime novels have remembered the long tradition of the sensation novel from which they sprang and have bit by bit become more and more like the ordinary novel of their day with an extra of crime added. Look at the books of Dick Francis, of Lionel Davidson, of Mary Kelly, of Ruth Rendell.

It is a development I myself welcome, and indeed hope I am part of when I take to fiction. It seems to me that as crime stories have managed to use characters that are less and less cardboard they have contrived both to keep the telling tug of the whodunnit and yet to be able to say as much, or nearly as much, as the novel proper. I think of books by P. D. James, Peter Dickinson, Reginald Hill, Celia Fremlin and June Thomson (I could think of others) and I rejoice.

Crime stories while still acknowledging that they exist first to entertain, that they are written for the sake of the reader and not primarily for the sake of what the writer has to say, have contrived over the years, and I believe will succeed in the years to come yet more, to have their say, to make their comments on our world as it actually is and on the way we mess it about. And at the same time, because they are entertainment, they have kept to the form expected of them and have, with exceptions that illustrate the rule, given their readers a happy ending, have asserted once more that justice ought to be done, have reaffirmed not simply our need for order in the chaos rising round us but that order can be, if ever so little, if only for a while, attained.

The Authors

JULIAN SYMONS is the author of *Bloody Murder,* a history of crime writing (Faber, 1972; Penguin Books, 1974) and numerous crime novels, among which *The Colour of Murder* (Collins, 1957. op; Fontana, 1966, op.) won a Crime Writers Association Golden Dagger and *The Progress of A Crime* (Collins and Fontana, 1960. op.) an Edgar Allan Poe award from the Mystery Writers of America. He was crime books reviewer for *The Sunday Times* from 1958 to 1968 and has also written historical studies and biographies, of which the latest is a study of Poe, *The Tell-tale Heart* (Faber, 1978).

REGINALD HILL is Senior Lecturer in the English Department of Doncaster College of Education. Author under his own name of nine crime novels that have earned high critical praise and of others under the name of Patrick Ruell, he has written a course of twenty lectures on crime fiction for the University of Sheffield extra-mural programme. He is contributing a number of critical assessments to a forthcoming reference work listing mystery story authors, for publication in Britain by the St James Press and in America jointly by MacMillan and St Martin's Press.

COLIN WATSON is the author of *Snobbery with Violence* (Eyre and Spottiswoode, 1971; Magnum Books paperback, 1978), a study of the sociological aspects of crime fiction from the 1920s to the 1960s. He has also written a series of humorous crime novels centred on the fictional Lincolnshire town of Flaxborough, some of which have been televised by the BBC under the title *Murder Most English,* and a novel, *The Puritan* (Eyre and Spottiswoode, 1966).

P. D. JAMES is a senior civil servant in the criminal department of the Home Office. Since a late start in 1962 she has written seven crime novels of which two, *Shroud for A Nightingale* (Faber, 1973; Sphere, 1973) and *The Black Tower* (Faber, 1975) have won Silver Dagger awards from the Crime Writers Association. Her short story *Moment of Power* gained first prize in a contest sponsored by *Ellery Queen's Mystery Magazine* in 1967. She is one of the regular crime fiction reviewers contributing to *The Times Literary Supplement.*

MAURICE RICHARDSON has been reviewing crime fiction for *The Observer* since the spring of 1939, having landed in England the previous September with 200 detective stories on his back. From 1955 to 1967 he was also *The Observer* television critic. He had edited *Novels of Mystery from the Victorian Age*, an omnibus volume for Pilot Press (1945) and *Best Mystery Stories* (1967) for Faber. As Charles Raven he wrote a series of crime documentary stories for *Lilliput.*

TROY KENNEDY MARTIN was the creator in 1962 of *Z Cars* for which he also wrote the final episode in 1978. His original screenplays include *Kelly's Heroes* and *The Italian Job.* He wrote six episodes of the television series *The Sweeney* as well as the second *Sweeney* film. His novel *Beat on A Damask Drum* appeared in 1959 for John Murray.

H. R. F. KEATING has been crime books critic for *The Times* since 1967 and is author of *Murder Must Appetize* (Lemon Tree Press, 1975), a study of the detective stories of the 1930s, and editor of *Agatha Christie: First Lady of Crime* (Weidenfeld and Nicolson, 1977). As a fiction writer, he created Inspector Ghote, of the Bombay CID. He is currently at work on an illustrated biography, *Sherlock Holmes and His World.*

MIKE PAVETT is a crime fiction enthusiast who started reading the hard-boiled American writers in his early teens. He has worked as a writer, director and editor of documentary films and was a script consultant on the *Crime Writers* television series.

Index

Adams, Bernard 7
'Adventure – The Red-Headed League' 24, 34
'Adventure of the Carboard Box, The' 24, 28
'Adventure of the Naval Treaty, The' 24
'Adventure of the Priory School, The' 51
'Adventure of the Retired Colourman, The' 24
'Adventure of Silver Blaze, The' 37
'Adventure of the Yellow Face, The' 24
Affaire Lerouge, L' 15
After the Thin Man 92
Aird, Catherine 153
'Albert Campion' 73
Alibi 63
Allingham, Margery 57, 58, 59, 73, 76
Altick, Richard 28
Ambler, Eric 139, 147
American Friend, The 116
'Annabelle' 116
Applebee, James 10
'Archie Goodwin' 77
'Arsène Lupin' 45
Art of Simenon, The 106
Asphalt Jungle, The 96
At the Villa Rose 47
Auden, W.H. 74

Babcock, Dwight 79
Bagley, Desmond 154
Ballard, Tod Hunter 79
Banana Tourist 110
Bank Shot, The 119
Barbarians, The 116
'Barlow' 125, 126, 127, 128, 129
Barnes, Arthur 79
Battle Of Nerves, A 106
Bear Raid, The 152
Beardsley, Aubrey 23
Beastly Murder 111
'Beaumont' 91
'Beck' 137
Before The Fact 77
Beggar's Opera, The 10
Bell, Joseph 19
Bell, Josephine 153
Bennett 145
Bentley, E.C. 47
Berckman, Evelyn 145
Bergman, Andrew 153
Berkeley, Anthony 57, 77
'Berni Ohls' 98
'Bertie Wooster' 71
Big Knockover, The 92
Big Sleep, The 95, 98, 99
'Bill Quint' 88
Billion Dollar Killing, The 151
Black Mask 78, 79, 82, 87, 94

'Blackmailers Don't Shoot' 94
Blake, Nicholas 57, 76
Bleak House 15
Blood Relatives 134
Bloody Murder: from the detective story to the crime novel: a history 7
Blue Lamp, The 123, 124
Blunderer, The 114
Bonfiglioli, Kyril 119
Borges, Jorge Luis 145
Bow Street Runners 11, 12, 13
Bramah, Ernest 42
Brand, Christianna 153
'Brigid O'Shaughnessy' 83, 86, 89
Brothers Rico, The 103
Browning, Robert 75
'Bruno' 113–14
'Bunny' 43
'Bunter' 67, 68
Burnett, W.R. 96, 98
Busman's Honeymoon 66, 69
Butler, Gewndoline 154
Butler, John K. 79

Cain, James M. 96
Caine, Hall 22
Caleb Williams 26
'Canon Avril' 73
Carr, John Dickson 77
'Cask of Amontillado, The' 14
'Celita' 108
Chandler, Raymond 53, 76, 79, 80, 94, 98
'Charley de Lisle' 114
Charteris, Leslie 55
Chesterton, G.K. 45, 46, 47
'Chevalier C. Aguste Dupin' 14, 37, 39
Cheyney, Peter 59
Children's Hour, The 84
Childs, Ted 130
Christian, The 22
Christie, Agatha 48, 49, 52, 53, 60, 73
'Christie Opera' 152
Churchill Commando, The 150
Clark, Mary Higgins 150
Clegg, Tom 130
Coburn, James 98
'Coffin Ed Johnson' 121
Colette 103, 107
Collins, Wilkie 15, 16, 29, 33, 35
Collinson, Peter. See Hammett, Dashiell
Colour of Murder, The 144
'Columbo' 136
Comèdie Humaine, La 14
'Continental Op' 82, 87–89
'Cordelia Gray' 152
Cortez, Richardo 82
Cory, Desmond 145
'Count Fosco' 15
Crash of '79, The 152
Creasey, John 120
Crime Writers, television series and extracts from 6, 19, 43, 78, 79, 94, 96, 117, 123, 127, 134, 137
Crispin, Edmund 153

Cry Of The Owl, The 114
'Cultured Faun, The' 23

Dain Curse, The 82, 89, 98
Daly, Carroll John 78
Dancers in Mourning 73
Dancing Dodo, The 150
Dannay, Frederic See Queen, Ellery
'Dave Brandstetter' 154
Davidson, Lionel 155
Davis, Norbert 79
Day, J.W. 28
Day-Lewis, Cecil 76
Day of the Jackal, The 151
Death at the Dolphin 73
Death in the Forest 149
Death On the Nile 63
Death Under Sail 57
Decline of the English Murder 153
Deep Water 114
Defence of Poetry 26
Defoe, Daniel 10
'Derwatt' 117
Detection Club, The 45, 76
Detective, The 150
de Veil, Sir Thomas 11
Dickens, Charles 15, 30, 33, 35, 150
Dickinson, Peter 155
Digges, Dudley 82
'Dinah Brand' 88
Disintegration Of J.P.G., The 104
Dixon of Dock Green 122, 123, 124, 126
Don't Point That Thing at Me 119
Double Indemnity 97
Doyle, Sir Athur Conan 17, 19–40, 21, 27, 50, 154
'Dr Gideon Fell' 77
'Dr Jervis' 42
'Dr Thorndyke' 42
'Dr Watson' 34, 35, 38, 39
Dragnet 121

Edalja, George 39
Edith's Diary 111, 117
Eighteen Nineties, The 25
'87th Precinct 121
Eleven 113
'Elihu Willsson' 88
Ellery Queen Mystery Magazine 77
Ellin, Stanley 141, 12, 143
End of Solomon Grundy, The 144
English Common Reader, The 28
Enter a Murderer 73
Erdman, Paul 151
'Eric Lethridge' 128

Farewell My Lovely 98
Fashion in Shrouds, The 73
'Father Brown' 45, 46
Fatty Arbuckle case 80
Ferrars, Elizabeth 153
Ferris, Paul 150
Fiction and the Reading Public 27
Fielding, Henry 11, 12
Fielding, John 11, 12
Five Red Herrings, The 69
Fleming, Joan 145

Fletcher, David 145
Flowers for the Judge 73
Follett, Ken 152
Forsyth, Frederick 151
Francis, Dick 155
'Frank Friedmaier' *109*
'Fred Pyall' *128*
Freeling, Nicolas *119*
Freeman, R. Austin *42*
Fremlin, Celia 154
'Fu Manchu' 55

Gaboriau, Emile 15, 16, *17*, 33, 35
Gardner, Erle Stanley 94, *95*
Gardner, John 150, 152
Garfield, Brian 137, *146*, 154
Garnett, Tony 129, 130, 131
Gaudy Night 71
Gay, John 10, *11*
'General Fentiman' 69
'Gerald' 116
Get Carter 118, 119
Ghost of Thomas Penry, The 152
'Gideon of the Yard' 120
Glass Cell, The 115
Glass Key, The 82, 86, 89, *90*, 92, 93
Godwin, William *26*, 31
'Gold Bug, The' 14
Graeme, Bruce 59
'Grave Digger Jones' 121
Greene, Graham 111–12
'Guild' 92
'Gutman' *82*, 89
'Gutting of Couffignal, The' 86
'Guy' 113

Haggard, William 147
Hammett, Dashiell, 78, *79*, 80–94, *81*, 98
Hansen, Joseph *154*
'Harriet Vane' 69, 71
Have His Carcase 68, 69
Haycraft, Howard 7
'Hazel' 115
'Hazell' 154
Hellman, Lillian 82, *84*
Hemingway, Ernest 86
Henderson, Laurence 154
'Hercule Poirot' 60, *62*, *63*
High Sierra 96, 98, *99*
Highsmith, Patricia 100–2, 111–117, *112*, 143
Hill, Reginald 20, *141*, 155, 156
Himes, Chester *121*
History and Remarkable Life of Jack Sheppard, The 10
History of the Life of the Late Mr Jonathan Wild the Great, The 11
Hopkins, John 134
Horler, Sydney 55
Hornung, E.W. *43*, 55
Hot Rock, The 119
'House Dick' 86
House of the Arrow, The 47
Household Words 15, 29, 33
Hume, Fergus 16
Hunter, Evan (Ed McBain) *121*, 134, 154
Huston, John 82

Iles, Francis. *See* Berkeley, Anthony
Innes, Hammond 154
Innes, Michael 76, *77*, 153
'Inspector Baynes' 33
'Inspector Bucket' 15
'Inspector Ghote' 120
'Inspector Hanaud' 47
'Inspector Parker' 67

'Ja Ja' 106
Jack Havoc' 73
Jack the Ripper *34*, 47
Jackson, Holbrook 25, 26
James, Henry 91
James, P.D. 64, 152, 155, 156
'Jeeves' 68
'Joel Cairo' *82*, 89
Johnson, Lionel 23, 25
Johnson, Nunnally 84
Jones, Elwyn 126, 134
Julia 80

Kahn, Joan 154
Keating, H.R.F. 6, 120, 138, 156
Kelly, Mary 155
Kemelman, Harry 153
Kenyon, Michael 139
Knox, Ronald *47*, 55, 76
'Kojak' 129, 134, *136*
Kale, Duncan 154

Last Seen Wearing 120
Lathen, Emma 153
Laughing Policeman, The 137
Laura 148
Law and Order 128, 129, 130
Leavis, Q.D. 27
Leblanc, Maurice 45
'Lecoq' 15–16
Lee, Manfred B. *See* Queen, Ellery
Lemarchand, Elizabeth 153
Levin, Ira 152
Lewis, Sinclair 86
Lewis, Ted *118*
Liberty Bar 106
Lippincott's Monthly Magazine 22
Little Caesar 96
Locked Room, The 137
Lodger, The 47
Long, Goodbye, The 98
Loo Sanction, The 146
'Lord Peter Wimsey' 55, 59, *67*, 69, 71
'Louis Carlyle' 42
Love is my Profession 108
Lovesey, Peter *148*
Lowndes, Belloc 47
Lyall, Gavin 79, 94, 96

McBain, Ed. *See* Hunter, Evan
McCoy, Horace 79, 94
Mcdonald, Gregory *144*, 145
Mcdonald, Ross 79, *96*, 153
McLean, Alastair 154
'Madvig' 91
Magnet Of Doom 107
'Maigret' 98, 103, 104, *105*, 107, 119,
Making Hate 139
Malice Aforethought 77

Maltese Falcon, The 82, *83*, 89, 91, 93, 99
Man on the Balcony, The 137
Man Who Watched The Trains Go By, The 103
Marric, J.J. *See* Creasey, John
Marsh, Dame Ngaio *72*, 73, 76
'Martin Hewitt' 42
Martin, Ian Kennedy 130
Martin, Troy Kennedy 122, 156
Mason, A.E.W. *47*
Masterplayers, The 150
'Maud' 108
'Max Carrados' 42
'Melinda' 114
Mencken, H.L. *78*
Micah Clarke 31
Mirror, Mirror 141
'Miss Marple' *60*, *61*
'Miss Twitterton' 69
Mitchell, Gladys 153
'Mme Barrabas' *83*
Moll Flanders 10
Moonstone, The 15, 29
Morbid Taste for Bones, A 149
Morrison, Arthur 42
Mower, Patrick 130
'Mr J.G. Reeder' 59
'Mr Ricardo' 47
Murder Ahoy 60
Murder for Pleasure 7
Murder is Announced, A 61
Murder Must Adverise 68, 71
Murder of Maria Marten, The 13
Murder of Roger Ackroyd, The 63
Murder on the Orient Express 63
Murder on the Thirty-First Floor 137
'Murders in the Rue Morgue, The' 14
Mystery of a Hansom Cab, The 16, *17*
Mystery of Edwin Drood, The 15
'Mystery of Marie Roget, The' 14, 39

Narcejac, Thomas 106
Nathan, George Jean 78
'Ned Beaumont' 89
'Nero Wolfe' 77
Newman, Gordon F. 129, 130, 131
Newnes, George 30
'Nick Charles' 84
'Nightmare Town' 91
Nine Tailors The 67, 69, 71
'Noble Bachelor, The' 26
'Noonan' 87

Offence, The 134
O'Hara, Kenneth 152
Opening Night 73
Orwell, George 153
Outsider, The 152

Paget, Sidney *24*, 25, *28*, *31*, *32*, *37*
'Parker' 118
Parker, Robert B. 153
Patience Of Maigret, The 107
Patriot for Hire, A 150
Patterson, James 153
'Paul Madvig' 89
Pavett, Mike 7, 8, 42, 76, 94, 118, 134, 156

'P.C. 'Fancy' Smith' 125
'P.C. Jock Weir' 125
'Peachum' 10
Pedigree 107
Peel, Robert 13, 15, 33
Peppercorn Kill, The 252
Permissive Society 141
Peters, Ellis 149
Petrodollar Takeover, The 152
'Philip Marlowe' 99
'Philo Vance' 77
Pickwick Papers 30
Picture of Dorian Gray, The 22
Pinch of Snuff, A 141
Plotting And Writing Suspense Fiction
  117
Poe, Edgar Allan 14, 35, 37, 39, 40
Point Blank 118
Policewoman 134
Postman Always Rings Twice, The 97
Potter, Jeremy 148-49
Premier, The 110
Price, Anthony 149
Prisoner in the Opal 47
Private Eye 98
Professionals, The 133
'Professor Moriarty' 31, 32
Progress of a Crime, The 144
'Purloined Letter. The' 14
Purple Noon 115
'Pym's Publicity' 71

Queen, Ellery. 77, 78, 139

'Race Williams' 78
Rae, Hugh C. 119
'Raffles' 43, 44, 45
Ragge, T.M. 104
Rapist, The 139
Red Harvest 82, 87, 88, 93
Redcap 131
'Regan' 131, 133
Remarkable Case of Burglary, A 148
Rendell, Ruth 155
Richardson, Maurice 100, 156
'Richmond' 13
'Ripley' 116, 117
Ripley's Game 116, 117
Roadhouse Nights 89
Robards, Jason 80
Robertson, W. Graham 23
Rohmer, Sax 55
Rosemary's Baby 152
Rossiter, John 154
Rubinstein, Paul 152

Saint Valentine's Day Massacre 97
'Sam Spade' 83, 84, 86, 87, 89, 94, 99
'Sapper' 55
Satan met a Lady 83
Sayers, Dorothy L. 53, 55, 59, 64, 65,
  70, 77
Scenes in the Life of a Bow Street
  Runner, Drawn up from His Private
  Memoranda 13
Season of the Machete, The 153
Send No More Roses 139
'Sergeant Cuff' 15

Shannon, Dell 154
Shaw, Joseph 94
Shelley, Percy Bysshe 26
Sheppard, Jack 10, 11
'Sherlock Holmes' 17, 19, 20-41 36, 38,
  39, 50-51, 154
Sign of Four, The 22, 30
Silver Bears, The 152
Simenon, Georges 98, 100-110, 101,
  105, 117
Simon, Roger L. 153
'Simon Templar' 55
'Simple Art of Murder, The' 53, 76
Sinclair, Andrew 150
Sinclair, Michael 150
Sjowall, Maj 137
Skinner 119
Slater, Oscar 39
Smiles, Samuel 28
Snow, Lord 57
'Socrates Smith' 59
Softly Softly 123, 127, 128, 129, 134
Special Branch 30
Stain on the Snow, The 109
Stark, Richard 118, 119
Starsky and Hutch 134, 135
Steel Spring, The 137
Stern, Richard Martin 139
'Steve Carella' 121
Stinson, Herbert 79
Stoddart, J.M. 22
Stout, Rex 77
Strand Magazine, The 17, 30, 31, 35,
  42, 50
Stranger Is Watching, A 136
Strangers on a Train 113, 114
Streets of San Francisco, The 136
Striptease 108
Strong Poison 68, 69
Stubbs, Jean 148, 154
Study in Scarlet, A 18, 22, 24, 30, 34
'Superintendent Alleyn' 73
Sweeney, The 130-33, 131
Symons, Julian 7. 80, 143, 156

Tale of Two Cities, A 20
Talented Mr Ripley, The 115, 117
Tales of Detection 64
Tanous, Peter 152
Target 133
Taylor, Eric 79
'Ted Shane' 83
'Ted Willis' 124
'Tell-tale Heart, The' 14
Theta Syndrome, The 152
They Shoot Horses, Don't They? 94, 95
Thin Man, The 82, 91, 92, 93
This Story Of Yours 134
This Sweet Sickness 116
Thomson, June 154
Thoreau, Henry David 26
Those Who Walk Away 102
'Thou Art The Man' 14
Three Act Tragedy 48
Thurber, James 91
Tiger in the Smoke, The 73
'Tom Ripley' 116, 117, 118
Towering Inferno 139

Trent's Last Case 47
'Trevanian' 146
Trevor, Elleston 152
Trevor, Ralph 59
True and Genuine Account of ...
  Jonathan Wild, A 10
'Tulip' 85
Two Faces of January 116

Uhnak, Dorothy 135, 152
Underwood, Michael 141
Unnatural Death 69
Unpleasantness at the Bellona Club,
  The 69

van de Wetering, Janwillem 152
'Van der Valk' 119, 120
Van Dine, S.S. 77
'Vautrin' 14
Verne, Jules 26, 34
'Victor Van Allen' 114
Vidocq, Eugène François 13, 14

Wahloo, Per 137
Wainwright, John 146, 147, 150, 154
Wallace, Edgar 56, 57, 59, 104
Wambaugh, Joseph 134, 154
Watson, Colin 48, 156
'Watt' 127
Waugh, Hillary 120
Webb, Jack 121
Wells, H.G. 26
Werewolf Trace, The 152
West, Nathanael 92
Westlake, Donald. See Stark, Richard
Wharton, Edith 86
Wild, Jonathan 8-11, 9, 14
Wilde, Oscar 22
Wilder, Billy 97, 98
Williamson, Frank 127
Willis, Lord (Ted) 123, 127, 129, 150
Wilson Colin 152
Wilson, Jacqueline 139, 140, 145
Window Over The Way, The 103
Wings of the Dove, The 91
Woman in White, The 15
'Wynant' 92

Yellow Dog, The 104
Yorke, Margaret 145
Yuill, P.B. 154

Z Cars 122, 123, 125, 126, 132, 134

Acknowledgments

ARROW BOOKS Margaret Yorke, page 145
ASSOCIATED PRESS Raymond Chandler, page 98
ATV NETWORK LTD Father Brown, page 46 right
BBC PHOTO LIBRARY *The Nine Tailors,* page 67, *Dixon of Dock Green,* page 124, *Z Cars,* page 125, *Softly, Softly,* pages 126 and 128, *Law and Order,* page 128, *Starsky and Hutch,* page 135
BBC TELEVISION *Kojak,* page 136, *Raffles,* page 43 below, Weston Gavin, page 117
BRITISH FILM INSTITUTE *The Adventures of Sherlock Holmes* (Twentieth Century Fox), page 38, *The Hound of the Baskervilles* (Hammer Films), page 39, *Raffles* (United Artists), pages 44 and 45, *Father Brown* (Columbia), page 46 left, *The Maltese Falcon* and *Satan Met a Lady* (both Warner Brothers) page 83, *The Thin Man* (MGM), page 93, *The Big Sleep* (Warner Brothers) (from Weidenfeld & Nicolson Archives), page 99, *En Cas de Malheur* and *La Neige Etait Sale* (both Miracle Films), page 108 and 109, *Strangers on a Train* (Warner Brothers) (from Weidenfeld & Nicolson Archives), page 113, *Plein Soleil* (Times Films, France), page 115, *Point Blank* and *Get Carter* (both MGM), both page 118
BRITISH LION (from Weidenfeld & Nicolson Archives) *Murder Ahoy,* page 60
CAMERA PRESS Agatha Christie (photo Bassano), page 49, Dorothy L. Sayers (photo David Higham), page 70, Patricia Highsmith (photo Reginald Gray), page 112
CINEGATE LIMITED *The American Friend,* page 116
CINEMA BOOKSHOP *The Glass Key* (Paramount), page 90, *The Maltese Falcon, High Sierra* (both Warner Brothers), both page 99
PETER DAVIES (from *Murder for Pleasure* by Howard Haycraft) Anthony Berkeley, Manfred B. Lee and Frederic Dannay, all page 77
EALING STUDIOS *The Blue Lamp,* page 124
ELLIOT & FRY Richard Austin Freeman, page 42, Monsignor Ronald Knox, page 47
EMI FILMS LIMITED *Death on the Nile*, page 62, *Murder on the Orient Express*, page 63
MARY EVANS PICTURE LIBRARY Jack the Ripper's victim, page 34
FIRST NATIONAL AND VITAPHONE PICTURE *Little Caesar,* page 96
FONTANA PAPERBACKS Ngaio Marsh, page 72, Rex Stout, page 77, Ross Macdonald, page 96, Mary Higgins Clark, page 150
MARK GERSON Julian Symons, page 143
VICTOR GOLLANCZ LTD Michael Innes, page 77, Maj Sjowall and Per Wahloo, page 137, Gregory Mcdonald, page 144, Anthony Price, page 149
SIR HUGH GREENE book covers of *Martin Hewitt Investigator* by Arthur Morrison, pages 42 and *813: a New Arsène Lupin Adventure* by Maurice Leblanc, page 45
BLANCHE C. GREGORY Dorothy Uhnak, page 152
GEORGE G. HARRAP & CO. LTD Joseph Hansen, page 154
WILLIAM HEINEMANN LTD (photo Theo Sanders) Janwillem van de Wetering, page 152
HODDER & STOUGHTON Donald E. Westlake, page 119
HUTCHINSON PUBLISHING Paul Erdman, page 151
MICHAEL JOSEPH Ted Lewis, page 118, Chester Himes (Photo Claire C. Lachance), page 121
KEYSTONE PRESS AGENCY LTD *Busman's Honeymoon* (MGM British Studios), page 66, Georges Simenon, page 101, Simenon with Maigret actors, page 105

ALFRED A. KNOPF H. L. Mencken, page 78
KOBAL COLLECTION (from Weidenfeld & Nicolson Archives) poster for *Double Indemnity,* page 97
STANLEY MACKENZIE COLLECTION facsimile of Conan Doyle's manuscript, page 18, Dr. Joseph Bell (photo Moffat), page 19, *Beeton's Christmas Annual,* page 22, Sidney Paget illustrations, page 24, 28, 31, 37, *Strand Magazine* covers, page 30, William Gillette, page 36, Eille Norwood, page 38
MACMILLAN LONDON Lillian Hellman, page 85, Jacqueline Wilson, page 139, Brian Garfield, page 146, John Wainwright, page 147, Peter Lovesey, page 148
RAYMOND MANDER AND JOE MITCHENSON THEATRE COLLECTION Charles Laughton, page 63
MANSELL COLLECTION Hungerford Stairs, Jonathan Wild, both page 9, ticket to Wild's execution, page 10, Sir John Fielding, page 12, Murder broadsheet, page 13, library ticket, page 17
NATIONAL PORTRAIT GALLERY, LONDON John Gay, page 11, Aubrey Beardsley by J. E. Blanche, page 23
PAN BOOKS Dashiell Hammett, page 81, Ed McBain, page 121, Ted Willis, page 127
PENGUIN BOOKS John Dickson Carr (photo Tom Blau), page 77, Erle Stanley Gardner, page 95, Nicolas Freeling, page 119, Stanley Ellin (photo Jerry Baur) page 142
POPPERFOTO Sir Arthur Conan Doyle, page 27, Agatha Christie, page 52, Margery Allingham, page 58, soup kitchen, page 97
RADIO TIMES HULTON PICTURE LIBRARY long song seller, page 8, Jack Sheppard, page 11, Bow Street runner, Henry Fielding, both page 12, Eugène François Vidocq, Edgar Allan Poe, both page 14, Wilkie Collins, policemen, both page 15, policeman, page 16, Sir Arthur Conan Doyle, page 21, William Godwin, page 26, Reichenbach Falls by Paget, page 32, G. K. Chesterton (photo Howard Coster), page 46, A. E. W. Mason, page 47, Edgar Wallace (photo Sasha), page 56, Dorothy L. Sayers, page 65, Chicago massacre, page 97
RANK FILMS *They Shoot Horses Don't They,* page 95
H. ROGER VIOLLET Emile Gaboriau, page 17
ROUTLEDGE & KEGAN PAUL from *Encyclopaedia of Mystery and Detection* by Chris Steinbrunner and Otto Prenzler) *Mystery of Hansom Cab* cover, page 17, Dr. John Thorndyke by H. M. Brock, page 42
W. H. SMITH station bookstall, page 29
TATE GALLERY, LONDON W. Graham Robertson by Sargent, page 23
THAMES TELEVISION Van der Valk, page 120, *The Sweeney,* page 131
TORRINGTON DOUGLAS *A Murder is Announced,* page 61
TV TIMES Anthony Valentine and Christopher Straul in *Raffles,* page 43, *87th Precinct,* Jack Webb, both page 121, *Columbo, Streets of San Francisco,* both page 136
UNITED ARTISTS *Bank Shot,* page 119
UNIVERSITY OF CALIFORNIA, LOS ANGELES RESEARCH LIBRARY DEPARTMENT OF SPECIAL COLLECTIONS (from Weidenfeld & Nicolson's Archives) *Black Mask* dinner, page 79, Raymond Chandler, page 94
WEIDENFELD & NICOLSON Joseph Wambaugh, page 154
CHARLES YOUNG Reginald Hill, page 141.

Acknowledgment is also due to the following:

BRITISH MOVIETONEWS LTD for transcription from film on Sir Arthur Conan Doyle, page 19.